THE CASE FOR MAKE BELIEVE

OTHER BOOKS BY SUSAN LINN

Consuming Kids:
The Hostile Takeover of Childhood

THE CASE
FOR MAKE
BELIEVE

SAVING PLAY IN A
COMMERCIALIZED WORLD

SUSAN LINN

THE NEW PRESS

NEW YORK
LONDON

Published in the United States by The New Press, New York, 2008
Distributed by Two Rivers Distribution

LIBRARY OF CONGRESS CATALOGING-IN-PUBLICATION DATA

Linn, Susan.
    The case for make believe : saving play in a commercialized world /
Susan Linn.
        p. cm.
    Includes bibliographical references and index.
    ISBN 978-1-56584-970-9 (hc)
    ISBN 978-1-59558-449-6 (pb)
    ISBN 978-1-59558-656-8 (ebook)
    1. Play—Psychological aspects.   2. Advertising and children.   I. Title.
BF717.L56 2008   2007042435
155.4'18'—dc22

The New Press publishes books that promote and enrich public discussion and
understanding of the issues vital to our democracy and to a more equitable world.
These books are made possible by the enthusiasm of our readers; the support of a
committed group of donors, large and small; the collaboration of our many partners
in the independent media and the not-for-profit sector; booksellers, who often
hand-sell New Press books; librarians; and above all by our authors.

www.thenewpress.com

Composition by NK Graphics, A Black Dot Group Company
This book was set in Fairfield LH Light

For my husband, Cliff Craine, with love

Contents

Part Three
The Realities of Make Believe: Play and Cultural Values

Acknowledgments

The ideas and experiences explored in this book represent a journey spanning many years. I have been fortunate to have received encouragement and guidance from an array of remarkable people along the way.

Most of what I know about children and therapy I learned from William Beardslee, who supervised my work at Boston Children's Hospital and has remained a friend, colleague, and mentor. Most of the rest I learned from Andrea Patenaude. Fred Rogers took an interest in my work in 1968 and I will always treasure my subsequent relationship with him and with Family Communications, his production company. My work at the Media Center of Judge Baker Children's Center affords me the ongoing privilege of benefiting from the wisdom, integrity, and kindness of its director, Alvin F. Poussaint. The Campaign for a Commercial-Free Childhood is based at Judge Baker and I'm grateful to its president, John Weisz, the trustees, and staff for supporting our mission.

My most recent thinking about play has been greatly influenced by four friends and colleagues: Diane Levin, Sally Jenkinson, Joan Almon, and Nancy Carlsson-Paige. Sally and Joan read and commented on portions of this manuscript, as did Barbara Sweeny, who also provided her usual stellar administrative support, and Eily Pearl, Josh Golin, Allen Kanner, Sharna Olfman, Michele Simon, Celia Shapiro, Sherry Steiner, Lauren Case, Judy Salzman, and Susan Wadsworth. Judy, Susan, Linda Barnes, and Sharon Bauer talked me through some of my more thorny patches of writer's angst. Tim Kasser, Michael Rich, Steveanne Aurbach, Ellen Bates-Brackett, Kathy Hirsch-Pacek, Sally Lesser, Marissa Clark, Enola Aird, Amy Aidman, and Stephen Sniderman were generous with their time and expertise. Chris Kochansky helped me organize early drafts. Courtney Novosat was an excellent research assistant.

I was able to devote significant time to writing through the generosity of the John and Geraldine Weil Foundation and the A.L. Mailman Family Foundation. Many of the children whose play I describe are from the SPARK Center of Boston Medical Center and the Corner Co-op Nursery School. I am indebted to Martha Vibbert, director of SPARK, and to Rosie and Sajed Kamal, directors of the Corner Co-op, as well as to the staff and families at their respective institutions.

My parents, Anne and Sidney Linn, were remarkably supportive of my quirky childhood interest in ventriloquism and my subsequent career. Gerald Whitman, a gifted ventriloquist, taught me, among other things, to say p, b, and m without moving my lips. My mother made the original Audrey Duck. Subsequent Audreys have been made and modified by Malinda Mayer, Karen Larsen, and Chris Godin. Karen Motylewski has been an anchor and sounding board through all the permutations of my work, as well as a great friend. Suzanne Gassner taught the first psychology course I ever took and opened up a whole world of wonder to me.

My editor, Ellen Reeves, believed in this book long before I did and is a delight to work with. My agent, Andrew Stuart, made the moral argument that convinced me to expand its focus. Thanks, also, to Jennifer Rappaport and the staff at The New Press for their unfailing dedication and professionalism.

Special thanks to my family—to Marley and Isabella Craine for their inspirational play, to Josh and Michele for joining in, and to Sasha for helping me remember what's really important. My husband, Cliff Craine, has always known who my puppets really are and was endlessly patient about reading and talking through more drafts of this manuscript than is reasonable for any human being to have been subjected to. I couldn't have written it without him.

THE CASE FOR
MAKE BELIEVE

Introduction

I am a woman of a certain age who talks to a duck. And get this: the duck talks back. Between us, we tell the truth. Without me, the duck can't talk. Without the duck—well, I can't imagine being without the duck. She has been in my life practically forever.

The duck is a puppet named Audrey. She is simultaneously me and mine. She's undergone numerous incarnations, but at the moment she is made of rust-colored cloth, a soft yellow beak, button eyes, and brown yarn braids flecked with a multitude of colors. Unlike me, she used to be a blonde. What emerges from her mouth is me, unconstrained by particulars like height, weight, expectation, and social convention. Speaking through Audrey frees up my deepest self and, in doing so, brings to light feelings, thoughts, and perceptions that might otherwise remain buried, or that I might not even know that I have. It is through Audrey that I have always experienced my most satisfying play. Because of her, I've spent most of my adult work life engaged in playing with and for children, thinking about the meanings of play, and working to ensure its survival.

At the age of six I developed an admittedly quirky and life-long interest in ventriloquism, which was spurred along by the unexpected gift of a sock puppet from a family friend. As an adult, I became a children's entertainer, performing live in venues ranging from street corners all over Boston to the Smithsonian. My puppets and a burgeoning fascination with child development eventually led me to the late Fred Rogers, who took an interest in my work. I appeared occasionally on *Mister Rogers' Neighborhood* and worked with his production company, Family Communications, to create video programs about difficult issues for children.

What fascinated me most about my puppets was the freedom of expression they afforded me and the ways that children confided in them when we chatted spontaneously after a performance. I began to think about their value as a tool for therapy and convinced Boston Children's Hospital to hire me as a puppet therapist, helping children use interactive puppet play to cope with illness and hospitalizations. In 1990, I completed a doctoral program in counseling psychology at the Harvard Graduate School of Education. In 1994, I came to work at the Media Center at Judge Baker Children's Center in Boston, where I am today. The Media Center's mission is to work with media to promote the health and well-being of children and to counter the media's negative effects.

It became clear by the late 1990s that we couldn't talk about media effects without talking about marketing and commercialism. That's when some colleagues and I founded the Campaign for a Commercial-Free Childhood (CCFC). Housed at Judge Baker, CCFC is a national coalition devoted to addressing commercialism in the lives of children. I've become an advocate and activist working with others to mitigate the harmful effects of commercial culture on children, including its powerful threat to make believe. My childhood experience and my years of working with children have instilled in me an awe bordering on reverence for the human capacity to play and its profound link to health, for ourselves and for society.

Play is so fundamental to children's health and well-being—and so endangered—that the United Nations lists it as a guaranteed right in its Convention on the Rights of the Child.[1] For children in the third world, societal horrors such as exploitation through slavery, child conscription, and child labor deny children their right to play. In the United States and other industrialized nations, seduction, not conscription, lures children away from creative play.

Lovable media characters, cutting-edge technology, brightly colored packaging, and well-funded, psychologically savvy marketing strategies combine in coordinated campaigns to capture the hearts, minds, and imaginations of children—teaching them to value that which can be bought over their own make believe creations.

In a culture where glitz is mistaken for substance and pundits tout the bells and whistles of technology as a panacea for most of life's ills, children more than ever need the time, space, tools, and silence essential for developing their capacities for curiosity, creativity, self-reflection, and meaningful engagement in the world. Yet in today's United States, society on all levels conspires to keep children from playing; in a market-driven society, creative play is a bust. It just isn't lucrative.

One major reason that creative play is not a moneymaker is that the satisfactions gleaned from it rely more on the person playing than on what's being played with. Children who play creatively find multiple uses for objects. They can transform a blanket into a tent one day and a cave the next. A stick can be a magic wand, a sword, a lightsaber, or a mast for a schooner.

The toys that nurture imagination—blocks, art supplies, dolls, and stuffed animals free of computer chips and links to media—can be used repeatedly and in a variety of ways. When it comes to make believe, less really is more. In the United States, this means that nurturing creative play is inherently countercultural. It's a threat to corporate profits.

Today's children are bombarded with messages designed to convince them that the key to happiness and well-being lie in the acquisition of brands, and the things that money can buy. Yet my colleagues who research that sort of thing find that what makes us happy are the more ephemeral pleasures of life—like relationships and job satisfaction. Adults and children with more materialistic values are actually less happy than those less invested in the things money can buy.[2]

If we truly believe that purchased products will make us happy, we get caught in a commercially constructed vicious cycle that goes like this: We buy a thing because we believe it will make us happy. And what happens? It doesn't. But if we believe that things will make us happy we buy another bigger, better—or even just plain different—thing. Yet we still aren't happy. So we buy another thing. And on it goes. Profits are built on convincing us and our children that happiness lies in our next purchase. That's why the electronic wizardry characterizing today's best-selling toys makes for great advertising campaigns. They *look* like fun. But they are created with a kind of planned obsolescence. They aren't designed with the goal of engaging children for years, or even months. They are designed to sell. If interest wanes, so much the better—another version of the toy will soon be on the market.

In my previous book, *Consuming Kids*, I describe how the onslaught of commercial marketing and our love affair with technology undermine children's capacity for, and inclination toward, creative play. In this book, instead of focusing just on what's wrong, I focus on what's possible—on the astonishing depth of feeling, self-reflection, and learning that flourish when children are allowed to generate make believe.

This book is about my experiences of why and how children play; why and how play is in danger of extinction; why it's essential for all of us to prevent its demise and how we can do that. Throughout, I share my observations of children at play. At its heart are stories about children with whom I've worked who use make believe to cope with the greatest of human challenges, including life-threatening illness, death, and loss. I've included these more in-depth explorations because I believe that bearing witness to children who play joyfully and constructively even in the worst of times is necessary to understanding play as a fundamental component of living a meaningful life and essential to mental health.

My goal in writing this book is to make a case for make believe at a time when its existence is terribly threatened—to share a lifetime of wonder at young children's depth of feeling and at how their capacity to engage naturally and spontaneously in pretend play gives voice to inner experience, allowing them to wrestle actively with life's challenges. It's for anyone who cares about children. My primary hope is that my experience will encourage you to ensure that the children in your life, and the children whose lives you affect, have time and space for creative play. I hope they play with friends. I hope they play by themselves. I also hope that when possible, and in your own way, you will play with them.

PART ONE

The Case for Make Believe

Why Play?

Defending Pretending

The Necessity of Make Believe

A four-year-old girl sits alone on a hospital bed. One railing is down. She dangles her feet over the side and clutches a worn-out stuffed monkey as she watches me come in. The next day she will be wheeled away from her parents, heavily medicated, and taken to a darkened room with no windows. She will lie on a table surrounded by machines. Adults in masks and gowns will strap her down and congregate around the lower part of her body, which will be screened from her view—she will not be able to see what they do to her. After a few hours of drifting in and out of sleep, she will feel a rush of heat inside her body and something pressing down hard at the top of her thigh. Finally she will be reunited with her family.

She is expecting me. Her mom and the nurse have told her that the puppet lady would be coming to talk to her about her upcoming cardiac catheterization—a diagnostic procedure during which doctors will snake a tube through one of the arteries leading to her heart. She stares at me silently as I sit down in a chair next to her bed.

"Hello," I say. "My name is Susan and I have some puppets.

I have puppets for you to use." I hand her four small animal puppets, including a rather benign-looking dog dressed as a doctor and a green felt dragon with a large mouth and pointed teeth. "And I have puppets for me to use too."

I pull out my all-time favorite puppet, Audrey Duck. Constructed of soft, brightly colored fabrics, she has brown yarn braids, button eyes, and a soft yellow beak. "I come and talk to kids in the hospital," I continue, slipping Audrey on my hand. "Sometimes we talk about the hospital and sometimes we talk about other things." Audrey looks carefully at the little girl and then looks at me. "Who's that girl?" she asks. "She looks nice."[1]

I am a ventriloquist who became a psychologist. I create worlds with my puppets and through them I can enter the worlds that others create. My work is play. For over thirty years I have played with all sorts of children experiencing all sorts of challenges, from facing the first day of kindergarten to coping with abuse or life-threatening illness.

My experiences with children are probably not like yours. Many of the children I see are grappling with physical or emotional pain that is unusual in twenty-first-century America. That I have spent countless hours engaging children in puppet play is also unusual. But what I've learned from my work is universal—even very young children are capable of passionate emotion, including love and rage, although they may not have the words to identify or articulate their feelings. I've learned that they are often attuned to the slings and arrows of the adult world, including stress and trauma that we hope they are too young to experience or be affected by. I have learned that play is healing. And I've come to recognize it as an essential building block for living a meaningful life.

I have been immersed so long in exploring the relationship of play to children's experience that it's sometimes hard for me to believe everyone is not as passionate about it as I am. But I am rescued from this myopia whenever I leave my office. When I bring play into a conversation I find that most people's eyes glaze over. I imagine they're thinking, "But play is so frivolous. Why should I even care about it?"

Why indeed? I attended a celebration recently that was populated mostly by adults and just a few small children. I was doing what grown-ups do at such occasions—laughing and talking with friends and family—when I felt something brush by my leg and looked down to see two small girls weaving in and out of the crowd. "Sister, sister," one cried to the other, "the witch is coming! Run! Run!" Intent on their fantasy, oblivious to the adults around them, their exuberance and palpable joy was a wonder to behold. That it evokes such delight is reason enough to place play high on my list of passions. But there's so much more. The capacity to play is a survival skill.[2]

Most child development experts agree, for instance, that play is the foundation of intellectual exploration. It's how children learn how to learn. Abilities essential for academic success and productivity in the workforce, such as problem solving,[3] reasoning,[4] and literacy,[5] all develop through various kinds of play, as do social skills such as cooperation and sharing.

I appreciate and value these aspects of play, but my true passion lies elsewhere: in exploring how play is linked to creativity and to mental health. My particular passion is make believe, or pretend play, which I think of as creating fantasy characters, imagining different realities, and transporting ourselves to pretend worlds other than the one we live in. Children's make believe is rooted in their unique experience of people and events. When given the opportunity to play, it comes naturally to them and serves as an essential early experience of self-reflection and expression. It is a gift, both to children and to the adults who care for them, and can be a window into their hearts and minds.

When allowed to flourish, each child's pretend play is unique—like fingerprints. A four-year-old of mixed religious heritage speaks through a dog puppet to say, "My heart is Jewish, but the rest of my body is Christmas." A six-year-old facing surgery turns the same dog into a doctor. A five-year-old just back from a dentist's appointment tells it to "open wide." Another child transforms it into a mom kissing her child good-bye at day care. In another child's hands, with a different family experience, the dog as mother watches implacably as her child drowns. Some children pass up the dog completely, choosing to speak through a hippo, a dragon, or a cow. A few shun my puppets altogether during our sessions, preferring to draw, build, or make music.

Pretend play combines two wondrous and uniquely human characteristics—the capacity for fantasy and the capacity for, and need to, make meaning of our experience. By fantasy I mean imagination, daydreams, and the stories we may or may not share with others that design the future, reshape the past, make new things possible, and illustrate powerful feelings. By making meaning, I mean the drive to reflect on and wrestle with information and events so that they make sense to us, enrich us, and help us gain a sense of mastery over our life experience.

Pretend play thrives in the intersection between the inner world of fantasy and inner experience and the external world that exists in time and space. Unlike daydreams, or most of our interactions with other people, it exists neither wholly in the inner nor wholly in the outer world—but it can shape both. Children's make believe play allows them to bring to light dreams and fantasies that, once they are no longer held inside, can be examined and reflected upon, and even altered by someone else's input.

I feel an increasing sense of urgency—the kind of urgency that environmentalists feel about saving the rain forest—about preserving time and space for children to play. Next to love and friendship, the traits that play nurtures—creativity and the capacity for making meaning—constitute much of what I value most about being human, yet they have been devalued to the point of endangerment by the prevailing societal norms characterized by a commercially driven culture and bombardment of electronic sounds and images.

I've noticed in the past few years—an observation reinforced by my colleagues who study young children and preschool teachers I talk to—that I can no longer assume that children know how to play creatively. The children I see at the day-care center often begin our sessions by picking up animals or little people figures and reenacting the exact same cartoon violence so popular on television, bringing nothing of their unique experience to their play. With sometimes just a little effort, I can help children pretend if I talk for various characters, or ask open-ended questions, or introduce themes that I know are important to them. "Does it talk?" a three-year-old girl asks about a baby doll she has just been given. "Yes!" I answer and pretend that the baby is crying. "Ma-ma," the baby wails in my voice. The little girl opens her arms. She envelops the doll in a big hug, comforts it, and launches into an elaborate scenario in which the baby doll's parents get dressed and go to a party, leaving the doll with a babysitter. With great glee, she spends several minutes reenacting this scene with minor variations.

Yet children shouldn't have to be taught to play. When they are given the time and opportunity in the context of even a moderately nurturing environment, play comes naturally to them. Babies are born equipped to learn about the world through interactions with caring adults, with their own bodies, and with the objects, textures, sounds, tastes, and smells they encounter.

Given the importance of play to children's lifelong cognitive, social, and emotional health, one would think that we would do everything possible to preserve space for it in our children's lives. Yet the exact opposite is happening. Studies on how children spend their time suggest that the time children spend on creative, pretend play is diminishing. A recent survey on children's time use suggests that from 1997 to 2002, over the course of just five years, the amount of time that six- to eight-year-old children spent on creative play diminished by about a third.[6]

In spite of the researched links between play and learning, government policies such as No Child Left Behind promote rote learning at the expense of quality playtime even in kindergarten. Time allotted to recess—another in-school opportunity for play—has been severely diminished, or cut out altogether, all across the country. Nor are kids left with much time to play outside of school.

These days, parents who can afford to are enrolling even their youngest children in structured enrichment classes or organized sports. Even parents who stay home with their children and want them to have unstructured playtime complain that all the other kids in the neighborhood are busy with after-school sports and activities. Working parents without access to adequate, organized child care may rely on television to keep children occupied at home. And, in many neighborhoods, parents feel that their children aren't safe playing outside.

Babies arrive in the world primed to play. From the earliest days we join in that play when we mirror their gestures and sounds, allow them opportunities to sustain interest in their discoveries, and when we give them opportunities to rediscover what's familiar. Initially play manifests in movement, touch, and vocalization—in the sensory pleasure babies derive from exploring the world—in actions and activities that they repeat over and over for their inherent pleasure. I was changing my nine-month-old granddaughter's diaper when suddenly Isabella made a rather unusual grunting noise—like "hmpf!"—and looked at me expectantly. The funny thing was that she sounded exactly like her older sister being silly. Matching her tone as exactly as I possibly could, I grunted back. She smiled a little and grunted again. So we spent a few happy moments together making silly noises at each other just because we could.

At first, babies play by attempting to repeat sensual pleasures, master physical challenges, and investigate and test the principles of the physical world. That funny, frustrating period when babies repeatedly and deliberately drop toys, spoons, and everything they can get their hands on is really an exploration of gravity. Those endless games of peek-a-boo are actually manifestations of early grappling with a lifetime of departures and arrivals, of comings and goings, and about testing a newly formed understanding that people and objects exist even when they are out of sight.

I was lucky enough to be visiting a friend at the moment his seven-month-old daughter made an astounding discovery—her knees. Squealing with glee, she extended her arms to her father, expressing in no uncertain terms her desire to stand up. As each tiny fist gripped tightly to one of his fingers she pushed up from her toes, and straightened to a standing position. After a few wobbly, upright moments she began to squat, bending her legs slowly. Then, like an inebriated ballerina rising from a plié, she teetered up once more. Beaming with pride, she repeated the sequence again—and again and again and again.

Eventually she noticed a favorite toy kitten on the floor. Holding on with only one hand, wobbling even more ferociously, she began to reach for the kitten only to find that (1) it was too far away to grab and (2) it was at ground level. With great deliberation, she extended her free hand toward the cat. Tottering precariously, completely focused on her mission, she began the glorious process of bending—and was saved from an undignified tumble by her father's protective arm. She allowed herself a brief rest on the floor and, with joyful determination, began the process anew.

Babies don't have to be taught to play—they are natural sensualists and explorers—rather we *prevent* them from playing. I remember wandering around an ancient Buddhist temple in southern Korea on a glorious fall day, the grounds filled with families. I noticed a baby of about seven months—old enough to sit by himself but too young to be mobile—sitting in the middle of a rather dusty patch of bare earth. Clearly, he had been placed there by his doting family—mother, father, grandmother, grandfather—so that they could take a picture of him. While I don't understand Korean, it was pretty obvious from the gestures and interactions of the four adults that they very much wanted him to look up into the camera and smile. The baby, however, had a different idea. He was bent over, running his hands through the dirt. Intent, completely engrossed, he traced patterns with his fingers. Ever so slowly, he picked up some of the dirt and gradually let it sift through his fingers. His grandmother pulled at him, cajoled him, and pleaded with him to look up at his daddy, who had his camera ready for a big smile—but to no avail. Despite the best efforts of four determined adults, he would not abandon his sensual, scientific, and playful exploration of dirt.

Children develop at different rates, but at some time toward the end of their second year an extraordinary change takes place in their play. They acquire the amazing capacity to make something out of nothing. It's not just that they can hold the visual memory of important people and objects in their heads, but they have the power to conjure up images at will and alter those images in any way they please. This early experience of pretending lays the foundation for creating—and delighting in—whole worlds that no one else can see.

It's a uniquely human characteristic that in the first years of life we acquire not just the ability but the desire to invest ordinary objects encountered in daily life with new and idiosyncratic meanings. As children develop their capacity to pretend, inanimate objects may acquire proper names and come to life as companions, soothers, and even scapegoats.

They begin to cuddle dolls and stuffed animals like real babies and can pretend to give them bottles to suck, feed them, change their diapers, and put them to bed. They want to dress up in grown-up clothes and—literally—walk in our shoes. In other words, they begin to enrich their lives through pretending and to exercise their imaginations in what experts call "symbolic play" when they recognize and use a symbol of something as representing, and sometimes substituting for, the thing itself. Blocks become bricks, water becomes tea, and a giant box can be a cave, or a house, or a rocket ship. But even as they enthusiastically conjure cookies out of thin air, talk to people who aren't there, or turn sticks into magic wands, they still remain grounded in the "real" world.

At the age of two, one little boy I know became especially

attached to an ancient greenish gray brocade cushion that he called Cushy. After a year or so the brocade, which was already fragile, wore so thin that holes appeared. Cushy began to leave a trail of stuffing behind wherever he went. Yet the little boy was adamantly unwilling to retire Cushy to a shelf. Finally, surgery was required. All of the cushion's stuffing had to be removed. Cushy was deflated, but by no means defeated. In his flattened state he acquired button eyes and a yarn tail and spent the next few years being simultaneously loved, played with, and blamed for various transgressions.

Once they develop the capacity for simultaneously recognizing a cushion for both what it is and what it could be, children are able to alter the world around them to play out their dreams and hopes, fears and fantasies. When children are given the time and opportunity, they turn spontaneously to pretend play to make sense of the world, to cope with adversity, to try out and rehearse new roles. They also develop the capacity to turn to pretend play as a tool for healing, for self-knowledge, and for growth.

I'm not saying that children's make believe play is like instant replay. In fact, it's not necessarily, or even usually, a literal rendition of a particular event or situation; rather it embodies important aspects of their *experience* of particular events and people. As in a dream, their feelings, hopes, fears, and desires get all mixed up with themes, events, and people from real life. When twenty-two-month-old Sophie repeatedly puts her baby doll to bed by throwing it angrily in a crib, it's not—I happen to know—that she has ever been treated that way. I also know that at this point in her life she's not fond of going to bed and often puts up a struggle about it. She doesn't have the language to say to her parents, "I experience being put to bed as being rejected by you, and it makes me angry," but she's capable of having those feelings and she communicates them quite precisely through her play.

When Sophie plays like this in the presence of adults who love her, she allows them access to her experience of bedtime in a way that might help them help her navigate this difficult transition. But Sophie's play is helpful to her even when she plays by herself with no adult watching. In addition to expressing her feelings in an acceptable manner, she gets to re-create a situation about which she feels helpless (being abandoned in her crib—against her will—for her dreaded nap) and transform herself into a person of power. *She's* doing the abandoning, rather than being abandoned. *She's* walking away from the crib rather than being left lying in it. And she gets to repeat the scenario as many times as she wants!

Play like Sophie's is a fundamental component of a healthy childhood. It is inextricably linked to learning and creativity. The ability to play is central to our capacity to take risks, to experiment, to think critically, to act rather than react, to differentiate ourselves from our environment, and to make life meaningful. Children often use pretend play to reflect on their lives the way many adults use journal writing.

As children's ability to follow a story line increases, their play becomes ever more elaborate. They can use it to tell intricate stories themselves, and after a while they are able to assume characters and personalities other than their own.

While this book is rooted in my experiences using puppets for therapeutic interventions with children, it is not a how-to manual on play therapy. My therapeutic work with children— like the work of any therapist—is based on years of training, experience, and a solid foundation in principles of child development and psychology. Nor is it designed to encourage parents to plumb the depths of their children's fantasies for hidden neuroses. Most parents aren't trained as therapists. And it is irresponsible for parents—even those therapists among us—to think that we can engage our own children in therapy. We aren't objective enough, we love them too deeply, we are too invested in their future, and—like any parent—we find it hard to bear the ways we might have hurt them.

That said, parents can recognize the fundamental importance of pretend play. We can provide opportunities for our children to play, we can allow them to play alone, we can play *with* them, and we can let them generate the themes and stories they play about.

In the process of preparing to write this book I returned to my twenty-year-old daughter's old preschool, the Corner Co-op, because I wanted to spend time observing "regular" children—that is, children who are not coping with the extreme life challenges most of the kids I work with face. I also wanted to be with children in a setting that is supportive, nurturing, and play-centered, but not therapeutic in a clinical sense.

As at any good preschool, children at the Corner Co-op have an opportunity to explore the world through a whole range of play, including block building, sculpting clay, painting, climbing, looking at books, music, balls, puzzles, planting, and crafts projects. They play with water and sand, and whenever possible they spend time outside. There's also plenty of opportunity for pretend play and the equipment that facilitates it: dress-up clothes, a loft, a wooden structure on rockers, and a couple of large, carpeted wooden boxes that can serve as various habitats such as boats, houses, and caves. Because of my particular interests, I found my attention focused primarily on children when they were engaged in make believe.

The teachers at the Corner Co-op are masters at entering constructively into children's play without imposing their choice of themes, characters, and plot. Each day—just because they can—the children in their charge play out some of the most profound human struggles while simultaneously sorting through the more mundane tasks they face. With joy and seemingly boundless energy the children immerse themselves in themes of death, isolation, and aggression, even as they grapple with sharing, cooperation, and the properties of the physical world.

Make believe is a natural means of coping with deep fears and fantasies, even for children leading the most sheltered of lives. It can often seem quite gruesome and serves two purposes. It's a way for them to gain a sense of mastery over the things that frighten or overwhelm them. It's also a time when young children, working so hard to conform to exhortations to "be good," have a chance to give voice to their very human desires to express the unacceptable—anger, selfishness, meanness, and fear. The children engaged in make believe at the Corner Co-op are no different.

I am watching two little girls rummage through a trunkful of dress-up clothes until they find a red, yellow, and blue jester's hat with bells attached to its several peaks. They identify this as "Beth's favorite hat." One grabs the hat, and together they race over to Beth, one of the teachers. "My favorite hat!" she says playfully. "Can I have it?" "No!" they answer, giggling, as they run away. Clearly, it's an old game. As they make the rounds of the room, stopping at various play stations, the hat transforms. "It's a *bad* hat," one of them proclaims. "A bad hat," the other agrees, and they run around with it for a while until, effortlessly, they transform it into a baby and cuddle it for a while. Later they deposit the hat carefully under a climbing structure and begin a new game that centers on poison walnuts.

Meanwhile, two other girls are busy piling toy food onto little plastic plates. They race over to another teacher and offer him some pretend candy. He "eats" it and says, "Mmm, delicious." "Poison ivy lemon drops!" they shout, laughing. "Here," says one, thrusting a plastic cup in their teacher's hand. "Poison ivy lemonade! You're going to die!" They laugh hysterically and run away.

Throughout what looks like chaos to the uninitiated, amidst all of the exuberantly played-out death and destruction, the teachers remain simultaneously calm and engaged. When the children draw them into their play, the teachers let the children drive its content. In the context of fantasy scenarios where terrible things happen, when a child "dies" or a stuffed animal is killed off, the teachers express appropriate feelings like sadness and fear. In doing so, they become models for how to express feelings, even feelings that society may find unacceptable.

No one is ever allowed to really hit, or really hurt, someone else. The teachers never do the scaring. They let children play by themselves and in groups, and join in when invited. They do not impose their own stories and fantasies on what's being played out. They have helped children learn not to impose their own fantasies on others who choose not to participate. "We're bad dinosaurs," one boy says to another. "No, I'm not!" his friend replies. Nor do the teachers probe the children's fantasy play for deeper meaning, which is what a trained therapist might do. Rather, they provide a chance for children to use their imaginations to take them virtually any place they want to go—and only as far as they are ready to go. The children have at their disposal paints, blocks, puzzles, clay, and dress-up clothes, and they use these materials to express themselves. It's not therapy. But it's certainly therapeutic.

As a psychologist, I am particularly interested in the healing powers of play—the ways it leads to self-understanding and personal growth. But pretend play provides children with so much more than that. It affords them the opportunity to learn invaluable skills—to immerse themselves in experience, solve problems, create possibilities where none exist, learn what it's like to be someone else, and make something new from that which already exists. Isn't our future as a society dependent on those skills? Art, music, cures for disease, new technologies, the plots, themes, and language for poems, novels, songs, and plays, as well as resolutions for conflict, are all rooted in creative play. Yet, in the United States today, society on all levels conspires to keep children from playing.

2

Sold Out

Commercialism, Technology, and Creative Play

At a conference for early-childhood educators in Seoul a few years ago, I saw a film shot in India of children from terribly poor villages playing. The young filmmaker responsible for the footage was Haemoon Phyen, head of the Korean Institute for Old-Fashioned Children's Play, Songs, and Tales, who commented that he had memories of playing that way as a child. Feeling that the play he observed in his own country lacked the joyous, creative abandon he remembered from his childhood, he took his search abroad—and found what he was looking for amid these starkly impoverished villages.

I am not romanticizing the daily struggles of poverty or minimizing its dreadful toll on children. Yet, as the children in the film scavenged barren fields, turning sticks and rocks into toys, the richness of their play was unmistakable. Immersed as we are in the digital age, it's easy to dismiss Phyen's institute and its mission as quaint. But his work is actually acutely relevant and quite forward-thinking. Play—so central to health and well-being—was once children's default leisure activity, but we can no longer assume that to be true. Nor should we underestimate the ramifications of this shift. Play is essential to the development of creativity, empathy, critical thinking, problem solving, and making meaning.

Given what's at stake, don't we all have a moral, ethical, political, and social obligation to provide children with the time, space, and tools to generate play? Since our capacity to play is inborn and used to develop naturally, it seems strange that we now have to make a conscious effort to ensure children opportunities for make believe. But we do. In the reality of today's childhood, play and its essential benefits are lost unless we consciously choose to resist prevailing societal norms, work to change them, or both. It's not just that play is no longer supported by the dominant culture. It is being actively undermined.

As with most societal issues, the ongoing demise of play is rooted in several factors, all of which need attention. Lack of public funding for parks and playgrounds means less outdoor space where children can gather and play. Another factor is the sense—justified in some communities but not in others—that it's not safe for children to play outside. I repeatedly hear from parents who are able to be home after school that, even in neighborhoods equipped with safe play spaces, their children have no one to play with. Their neighbors' children are involved, by necessity or choice, in structured after-school programs.

Public schools, struggling with underfunding and bound by law to produce students who show demonstrable proficiency in math, reading, and science, focus their efforts on getting students through standardized tests, which tend to involve more memorization and less learning how to think. In the thrall of "teach to test," school boards view programs that promote play and creativity, such as recess, physical education, art, music, and drama, as expendable. Play is being eliminated from kindergarten, especially in poorer neighborhoods.[1] It is disappearing even in preschools where the focus is shifting to inculcating so-called academic skills such as memorization of letters and numbers and whose art projects consist primarily of pasting pre-cut turkeys, autumn leaves, Christmas trees, or menorahs onto construction paper.

For children of privilege, time spent in creative play is eroded by overscheduling, highly structured activities, team sports, and enrichment classes. Poor children spend more time watching television than their wealthier peers[2]—in part because they have less access to safe parks, playgrounds, and play spaces. Cheaper toys, found in megastores like Wal-Mart, Kmart, and Target, are often de facto promotions for media programs.

Across class divides, immersion from infancy in commercialized culture—manifest especially in electronic media and the things it sells—interferes with children's natural impulses for generating their own creations. The synergy between unfettered commercialism, the proliferation of electronic media, and other advances in media technology may generate corporate profits, but it's wreaking havoc with children's play.

Before I go any further, I should explain that I'm neither a Luddite nor a technophobe. As a psychologist and a children's entertainer, I have spent a significant portion of my adult life creating video programs designed to help children talk about difficult issues. As a young adult I appeared regularly on television programs in Boston, and worked on televised public service campaigns. I had the good fortune to be mentored by the late Fred Rogers, appearing occasionally on *Mister Rogers' Neighborhood* and producing, with his production company, video teaching materials about topics such as racism and child abuse. I do not find screen media to be inherently harmful. However, a serious threat to the health and well-being of children is the *business* of children's media and the marketing that drives virtually all of its production.

Research tells us that it is possible for thoughtful screen media to be a springboard for creative play.[3] In my own childhood, hours of make believe and an entire life's work were inspired by television and movies. I became enamored of Flash Gordon, a precursor to modern superheroes, through old movies serialized on television. He and Peter Pan both figured heavily into my pretend play. My interest in ventriloquism—which evolved into a vocation—began at the age of six and was inspired by watching the master ventriloquist Paul Winchell and his dummy Jerry Mahoney on the small screen. As an adult, seeing old footage from Burr Tilstrom's *Kukla, Fran and Ollie* show, I realized that one of my puppets—a boy lion named Cat-a-lion—has his roots in Tilstrom's creation Oliver J. Dragon, or "Ollie" as he was called.

I'm not arguing that children's lives would be better if only we could bring back programs from the 1950s. They were vehicles for all kinds of cultural stereotyping and sneaky marketing techniques. The portrayal of Indians as inept stooges in *Peter Pan*, in both the Disney film and the televised stage play, is racist. Wendy is a simpering wimp. I recently spent a nostalgic few hours laughing at the primitive special effects and melodrama in *Flash Gordon's Trip to Mars*, which was in movie houses in the 1930s and which I saw on television twenty years later. But it isn't funny that the only black character is a bumbling servant and the main female character, Dale Arden, who blasts off in a suit and heels, spends an inordinate amount of time in a dead faint, shrieking, or breathlessly cooing, "Flash! Oh, Flash!" at the hero's every move. The characters on *Kukla, Fran and Ollie* pushed brands like Whirlpool, *Life* magazine, and RCA throughout their program, as did the cast of the first children's television phenomenon, *Howdy Doody*.[4]

So it's not that the content of screen media was better when I was a kid. In some ways it was worse. There was, however, so much less of it. Today, children's exposure to screen media extends way beyond television or film. MP3 players, cell phones, and personalized DVD players all display media content targeted to children. Children are subjected to screens at home, in restaurants, at school, in their pediatrician's waiting room, in the backseats of minivans, in airplanes, and even in supermarket shopping carts. Explaining that screen media programming is now targeted at children in the interstitial moments of their lives—when they're between places—an executive at Nickelodeon quipped, "Nickelodeon is everywhere kids are."[5]

When J. Paul Marcum, the head of Sesame Workshop's interactive group, commented on his company's contract with Verizon to download television content onto cell phones, he denied that the venerated children's media company advocated selling cell phones to young children. Then he added, "But you can't ignore the convenience factor when people are in motion. A parent can pass back a telephone to the kids in the back of the car. And it's a device that families are going to carry with them everywhere."[6] According to the *New York Times*, cell phones are the new rattle.[7]

To understand the extent to which many of today's children are immersed in commercialized media culture, think about the children you know. How much time do they spend engaged with electronic media—most of which is commercially based? On average, children ages two to eighteen are "tuned in" about forty hours a week after school.[8]

Television is still the primary venue for advertising to children, but marketing on the Internet is escalating. Nickelodeon's Web site, Nick.com, took in $9.6 million between July 2004 and July 2005—more advertising revenue than any other Web site for either children or adults.[9] When the Kaiser Family Foundation looked at seventy-seven Web sites that food companies use to target children, they found that these sites received more than 12.2 million visits from children ages two to eleven in the second quarter of 2005.[10] In fact, as digital technology becomes more sophisticated, TV and the Internet are merging to become a whole new interactive media and marketing experience for children.

When screens dominate children's lives—regardless of content—they are a threat, not an enhancement, to creativity, play, and make believe.[11] If children are constantly in front of screens, when do they have time to explore and develop any thoughts, feelings, and ideas that media content might engender? Research suggests that the more time children have to nurture and develop their own interpretations, the more they are likely to move beyond the script they've viewed.[12]

In addition to replacing creative play as a leisure time activity, screen media is less apt to generate creativity and imagination than radio and books—which require more of us. Reading requires us to imagine both aural and visual images. Radio provides sound, but still necessitates that we imagine what the story looks like.[13] Screen media does all of that work for us and, in addition, seems to be an aid in remembering content—which may make it a boon to certain kinds of learning, but a bust when it comes to nurturing imagination.[14]

Compounding the problem is that DVDs, MP3 players, cell phones, TiVo, or other home recording devices that provide programming "on demand" make multiple viewings of the same program a new fact of children's lives. With the option of unlimited access, children are able to enter the world of their favorite characters and stories any time they want. They become able to recall the entire program practically verbatim—another detriment to pretend play. Even if we reread favorite books repeatedly (one of my guilty pleasures), we still have to use our imaginations to envision what the characters look and sound like, and our images may change or grow over time.

Here's how it works with screen media. When I was a child, Flash Gordon movies were serialized on television, but only occasionally. Disney's *Peter Pan* wasn't on television, and the TV adaptation of the Broadway play was broadcast annually for a few years. Instead of unlimited access to the media programs we loved, children had unlimited access only to our own imperfect memories of the stories and characters we saw on the screen. The only way I could satisfy my desire to immerse myself in the world created by screen versions of *Peter Pan* was to construct it myself. In a sense, I *had* to play. In the process, I could make Neverland my own.

The reality is that if I had been able to watch *Peter Pan* every day, I'm quite sure I would have done so. I'm glad it wasn't an option. There is no need to imagine anything about a story whose script and characters are indelibly imprinted in your memory.

When the first episode of the original *Star Wars* trilogy debuted in 1977, the thirty-somethings of today were able to see it only during its run in a local movie theater—home video players hadn't come out yet. By 1983, when the third episode was released, VCRs were increasingly common and the episodes were released on video a year later. Children now had unlimited access to repeated viewings of films and television programs.

Star Wars ushered in the now standard phenomenon of

marketing blockbuster movies through toys. In 1984, striking another blow against make believe, the Federal Communications Commission (FCC) deregulated children's television, making it possible to create children's programs for the purpose of selling licensed products, and within a year all ten of the best-selling toys had ties to some sort of screen media.[15] Today, the plethora of media-linked toys is another commercial phenomenon that inhibits creative play.[16]

Twenty years later in 2004, *SpongeBob SquarePants* brought Nickelodeon about $1.5 billion through sales of related food, toys, clothing, and other products.[17] About 97 percent of American children six and under own something—a doll, a stuffed animal, an action figure, bedding, or clothing—that features the image of a character from the media.[18] It is increasingly difficult to find any products for children—from food to toys—that are unadorned by media characters and logos. Even children's books are often media-linked.[19] "My third-grader drew a picture of Mad-Eye Moody from the Harry Potter series," a mother told me. "He'd read the books but hadn't seen the films. A girl at school saw the drawing and informed him that it was 'wrong.' When he told me about it, I tried to explain that Mad-Eye Moody was a made-up character—that there wasn't a right or wrong way to imagine him. But he wouldn't have it. "Yeah," he sighed, "but she's seen the movie!"

The girl who criticized the picture of Mad-Eye Moody didn't say that it was a bad drawing or even that his image of the character didn't agree with her image. She said that it was *wrong*. According to Dan Anderson, a noted researcher in media for young children, "Children are forming attachments with media images. [With every branded purchase], you've turned over part of your child's love to a giant corporation."[20] I would add that you've also turned over your child's imagination to corporate interests.

What were once tools for self-expression are now designed to remind children constantly of media programs and their products. Toys representing media characters steer children toward set internalized "scripts" from which it is hard to deviate.[21] Like the boy who drew the "wrong" picture of Mad-Eye Moody, I find I encounter surprising rigidity when I engage with children in make believe rooted in screen imagery and try to change the personalities of the TV or movie characters. They will create all kinds of inventive personalities with puppets—unless they're given a character with which they're familiar from the media. Then they usually stick to a rigid portrayal of the character exactly as it's seen on television or in the movies: a Cookie Monster puppet is always the Cookie Monster and does little more than consume cookies.

Adults do the same thing. When I give workshops on using puppets with children, I always bring a supply for participants to practice with. Most of the puppets I've collected over the years are generic animals or fantasy creatures, but I do have a few based on movies and television programs. When participants begin talking through the puppets spontaneously, I always see all sorts of wonderfully creative characters—except for whoever gets the Cookie Monster or some other TV character. These don't vary a bit from their media persona. In combination with repeated viewings that enable children to memorize scripts, such media-linked toys can be particularly deadening.

In addition to characters, the props used in media programs are also marketed to children—which further constricts make believe. Young fans of the Harry Potter books don't have to make the imaginative effort to transform sticks into magic wands when detailed replicas are available at toy stores. Because these toys are often heavily advertised, the message sent to both children and adults is not just that these props are better than children's own creations or that enjoyment of the film depends on owning them. The underlying message is that children will actually be unable to play without them.

It's a mistake to underestimate the powerful impact screen media and its commercialized accoutrements have on children—even on those whose parents limit television or on those too young to understand what they're seeing. After a recent talk in Charlottesville, Virginia, I met a mom whose two-year-old daughter watches no television at home. But after a beach vacation with extended family, she was exposed to Nickelodeon for the first time; all the other children in the house were watching, so she did too. "My daughter didn't seem to pay much attention to it," her mother said. "But then when we got home I notice that she'd added a new character to her doll house—Nick Junior. It was 'Nick Junior' did this and 'Nick Junior' did that. She even invented a character named 'Nick.com.' It's still going on and we left the beach a month ago!"

I've come to think of electronic media in the same way that I think about candy or junk food. Consuming it can be pleasurable, but too much isn't good for you. It can also be habit-forming. Most of it contains nothing essential to children's health and well-being. It's not recommended for babies. When children's diets are dominated by junk food, they are deprived of food that we know contributes positively to their growth and development. While junk foods may vary in their relative lack of benefit to children and are enjoyable treats, children get essential nutrients from other foods. It's easier to postpone children's access to candy than it is to limit it once they've started consuming it. And I think that's true for media consumption as well.

Of course, screen media and media-linked toys are not the only ways that commercial culture erodes creative play: so do most of the toys embedded with computer chips. Thanks to modern technology these come equipped with voices, sounds, and movement that deprive children of the opportunity to gain the essential experience of creating, exploring, solving problems, expressing themselves, and making meaning.

I once bought a doll online for a toddler without realizing that it was electronically "enhanced." When it arrived, I discovered that a battery could make the doll laugh, cry, gurgle, and do just about everything. In fact, the doll wouldn't even blink without a battery. Meanwhile, the hardware necessary to do all that made the doll's chest so rigid and heavy that it was uncomfortable for a young child to hold. All the characteristics that make baby dolls good toys for young children were missing. It couldn't be cuddled or hugged. Nor did it require a child to construct a voice, personality, or sounds—to talk, cry, and gurgle for the doll instead of passively observing it. Once I realized that it would add nothing to a child's fantasy life, I felt that, in good conscience, I couldn't give it to a toddler. So I presented it instead to an artist friend who creates art out of found objects and who, I'm sure, is putting it to good—if fairly bizarre—use.

One of the hottest toys during the 2005 holiday season was a doll called Amazing Amanda equipped with microchips that enable her, among other wonders, to ask for breakfast cereal and respond, when presented with a toy plate of microchipped macaroni and cheese, "Silly Mommy, that's macaroni and cheese." It has an internal clock that tells time, and differentiates times of the year. It is programmed, on request, to smile, and make funny and sad faces. It recognizes digitally equipped pizza. Amazing Amanda was called a "marvel of digital technology" in the *New York Times*[22] and was one of the top-selling toys that year.[23] It was advertised heavily on television and on Web sites like Nick.com. Amazing Amanda sold so well that it was no great surprise to find Amazing Allysen—Amanda's older sister—on the market the next year. But during that holiday season the "hot" toy was Butterscotch, a computer-enhanced pony similar in concept to Amanda. Allysen was nowhere near as popular as her younger sibling.[24]

It's not surprising that Allysen didn't sell as well. It's easy to see that most young kids who saw ads for Amazing Amanda would be enraptured. But there's a problem. She's not that much fun to play with day after day. Every programmed response uttered by Amanda deprives children of a chance to exercise their own creativity by speaking for her, by making up her voice and her responses. Some adult must have had a lot of fun thinking up things that she could do and figuring out how to make them happen—but not the children playing with her. One mother who bought Amazing Amanda for her eight-year-old daughter had this to say: "She was so excited when she opened the box at Christmas. And she played with the doll intensely for a few days. And then it kind of stopped. She takes her out occasionally, but, to tell you the truth, we call her 'Annoying Amanda' now."

If a child owned only one or two toys characterized by programmed responses, the threat to children's imaginative world would be minimal. The problem arises when preprogrammed toys dominate a child's playthings. "My four-year-old doesn't like plain old dolls," explains another mother. "She likes toys that interact with her." Yet "interactive" toys like Amazing Amanda aren't truly interactive—or rather, the interaction isn't equal. The toys are active and the children for whom they are designed are reactive. The creator of Amazing Amanda describes playing with it as leading "a child through play."[25] However, children who have been given adequate opportunities to play since infancy don't need toys to "lead" them.

This type of advertising, which promotes a mistrust of children's capacity to grow and develop naturally, without dependence on brands, is not unusual around children's toys and media. As I noted, the *New York Times* celebrated Amazing Amanda as a breakthrough in toy design; however, child development specialists were less dazzled and significantly more skeptical. A few days later the *Times* published a letter from Ed Miller of the Alliance for Childhood. Miller, quite astutely, pointed out that "dolls have always been able to 'talk' and 'show emotion,' through the power of the child's imagination. Those words and emotions spring from the child's experience of the world, not from a canned script programmed into voice-recognition software."[26] As Joan Almon, director of the Alliance, says, "A good toy is 90 percent child and 10 percent toy."[27] The more a toy contributes to the interactive process, the less effort a child makes to think creatively, to come up with solutions or act spontaneously—and the less benefit children derive from that toy.

A child playing with a simple stuffed fantasy creature gets to exercise imagination by creating a character—picking its age, gender, voice, personality, and movements, and even its species. A creature wearing a dress eliminates choice of gender. A creature in a ballet skirt, combat boots, or a crown narrows choice of identity. A creature representing a specific media character—like Elmo—eliminates the opportunity to create a personality. An Elmo enhanced with a computer chip that allows him to speak robs children of a chance to make up a voice and limits the situations they might imagine for that specific character and the responses they might invent. A toy like

Chicken Dance Elmo, Hokey Pokey Elmo, YMCA Elmo, or any of that series, in which a specific media character independently moves and makes noise, robs children of just about any play experience that could be valuable to them.

In *Consuming Kids*, I wrote about a 2002 visit to the Jewish Museum in New York City to see a show called "Mirroring Evil: Nazi Imagery/Recent Art." One of the most controversial pieces in the highly controversial exhibit was Zbigniew Libera's *Lego Concentration Camp Set*. At first glance, the classic, brightly colored box and the block construction beside it evokes endless hours of creative fun. Consistent with modern-day Legos, it's clear that the set is designed as a kit rather than a free-form collection of blocks. The picture on the box, which is carefully replicated in the construction beside it, suggests that the pieces enclosed make a particular construction that appears at first to be some kind of a fort or modern army encampment. Closer examination shows that, in fact, this apparently harmless children's toy contains the building blocks for a Nazi death camp—including skeleton-like figures that serve as the emaciated inmates.

Reviews of the show complained that it was an outrage to depict a death camp as a child's plaything. Certainly the notion of children building a model death camp for fun is horrifying. Some reviewers accused Libera of "contaminating" an excellent toy. In fact, I noticed a disclaimer from the manufacturer exhibited next to the doctored packaging, disavowing any endorsement of the artwork. But what intrigued me were the links between Nazi imagery and my concerns about how commercialism constricts children's play. The Lego set simultaneously *depicted* fascism (a death camp) and *was* dictatorial in its insistence that there was a single correct object to be built from the blocks. That construction toys and art materials are increasingly offered as kits also blights opportunities for children's creative expression. It's true that building with Legos has been a wonderful creative experience for children over the years, but the concentration camp piece reminds me of another disturbing trend in commercial children's toys away from nurturing creative play to fostering a more constricted experience. Legos, like other creative construction toys, are now often packaged as kits rather than as a free-form collection of blocks. The brightly colored boxes, and the instructions within, provide a compelling argument for a "right" way to put the blocks together. In recent years I've noticed this kind of rigidity often in the children I encounter.

As I sit on the floor of a hospital playroom with seven-year-old Annie, she reaches for a box of Lincoln Logs and dumps them out on the floor. In addition to the logs themselves, the set contains one plastic roof, one doorway, three window frames, and a set of instructions detailing exactly how to build three different structures. The original Lincoln Logs sets, from the 1930s, contained only logs: novice builders just left openings for the windows and doors. At that point the kits did not come with preconstructed accoutrements, so children could place the openings anywhere. Like modern versions of Legos, today's Lincoln Logs offerings come with instructions rather than a few suggestive pictures of multiple possibilities.

Keeping a rather anxious eye on the pictures, Annie tries to duplicate one of the detailed models on the page. Before she has it exactly right she places a plastic roof on top. It doesn't fit. We have not built the structure exactly to specification. Dismissing my suggestion that we build something of our own, she tries again to get it right. In fact, it's not clear to me that we could have created a structure much different from the three models. A building set that allows for creativity should contain lots of different-sized pieces: this kit contains only enough logs in just the right numbers to build only those structures depicted in the instructions.

If children are, from birth, provided mostly with kits and electronic or media-based toys they won't have a chance to learn how to enjoy or even approach challenges that call for imagination, experimentation, inventiveness, or creative problem solving—and we will stop providing those challenges. A worrisome consequence of a commercialized play environment is that we begin to distrust children's capacity for imaginative play. We start to believe that they aren't capable of generating constructive activity on their own. We and our children begin to think that their natural instincts aren't good enough and that they need the things corporations sell in order to occupy themselves constructively.

A childhood bereft of make believe, or open-ended play, deprives children of opportunities for developing their capacities for imagination and creative thinking. I was visiting a small children's museum recently, which was filled with wonderful exhibits designed to stimulate creative play. When we came to the art room, however, I noticed that the children were engaged in making pictures that involved pasting buttons on top of pre-cut construction paper stems. When I wondered aloud why they didn't provide a more open-ended experience, the director said sadly, "We tried that. The children just don't know what to do with the materials." It's disconcerting that institutions like children's museums now find themselves serving children who enter their doors without the skills or inclination to engage in open-ended creativity. In response, they are less likely to provide such activities, and children have lost yet another opportunity for creativity and self-expression.

If, as it seems, we are constructing a modern childhood

dominated by experience that promotes reactivity, conformity, and the notion that challenges have only one solution, then Libera's Lego death camp is an ominous portent. Creative play fosters divergent thinking, the capacity to think "outside the box," imagining ideas and solutions to problems that go beyond convention. Divergent thinking is a threat to totalitarianism. It is essential to democracy.

If we constrict children's opportunities for creative play from birth, they won't even begin to know how to generate new ideas, challenge existing norms, or revel in their own creativity. That's why perhaps the most troubling trend in a commercialized culture fraught with troubling trends is the media and marketing industry's all-out effort to get babies and toddlers hooked on screens and electronic gizmos from the moment they're born. What's at risk is no less than the development of essential life skills—including the essential capacities to look to themselves for generating amusement, and to soothe themselves when they are stressed.

3

Baby Scam

The False Promise of Screen Time for Infants and Toddlers

I am babysitting for twenty-month-old Marley and she misses her mom. As she stands on her changing table and I help her get ready for bed, her face begins to take on a pained look of "how can this be happening to me" outrage that gives way to grief. "Mama," she begins to cry, "Mama!" "Your mom and dad went out to dinner," I say. "And they'll be back again." This information brings a fresh round of tears, but then something surprising happens. Her sobs for "Mama" become interspersed with a kind of hiccoughed crooning. "It's okay," she says. "It's okay." She sounds just like her mom.

I am witnessing the mechanics of a wondrous and absolutely normal phenomenon—the process of a baby engaged in self-soothing. The capacity to turn to her internal resources for comfort—to call forth not just a memory of being soothed, but the internalization of a soothing voice repeating "It's okay"—is a marvelous gift for coping with the human conditions of despair and loneliness. Babies who, for whatever reason, don't have the experience of parental soothing may go through life without an essential life skill and may instead turn to outside forces such as food, alcohol, drugs, or compulsive behaviors in order to make themselves feel better in times of stress.

In recent years, babies—even babies with loving, giving, healthy parents—have begun to face another threat to gaining the capacity to self-soothe: videos, DVDs, computer software, and the products they license. By targeting babies, media companies are marketing not just programs and characters but lifelong habits, values, and behaviors. These companies are wiring dependence on media before babies even have a chance to grow and develop, and are simultaneously removing babies and toddlers further and further from the very experiences that are essential for healthy development. A steady diet of screen media deprives babies of opportunities to develop the inner resources to amuse themselves or soothe themselves without an electronic crutch. We seem bound and determined to raise a generation of children who are bored or anxious—literally uncomfortable—unless they are in front of a screen.

The media and marketing industries have been wildly successful in convincing parents that screen time is both beneficial to babies and essential to child-rearing. That both beliefs are false, and that science to date even suggests that screen time may be harmful to babies, does not seem to matter. It's a warped tribute to the power of advertising that the baby media industry is booming despite all evidence to the contrary and the public concerns of such respected advocates for children as T. Barry Brazelton, Alvin F. Poussaint, and David Elkind.[1] The American Academy of Pediatrics (AAP) actually recommends no screen time for children under two.[2] Yet almost 50 percent of parents believe that baby videos have a positive effect on child development.[3] By the time babies are two, 90 percent are engaged with screens for an average of an hour and a half per day,[4] with 14 percent spending more than two hours a day in front of screens.[5] Forty percent of three-month-old babies regularly "watch" television and DVDs for an average of forty-five minutes a day.[6] And 19 percent of babies under the age of one have a TV set in their bedrooms.[7]

While American children are seduced by glitz, glitter, and beloved media characters into forsaking make believe, adults are seduced into depriving them of it—mostly in the name of learning. We fork over billions of dollars each year on electronic media and gizmos claiming to teach young children, even babies, everything from the alphabet to manners. The Fisher Price Laugh and Learn learning phone for babies as young as six months—a battery-operated toy cell phone, sporting its own little screen—claims to do both.[8] Selling screens as educational exploits two vulnerabilities that seem to be common to many of the parents I meet today. They are concerned about academic success and they are horribly stressed. The latter is particularly true for single parents and families with two parents in the workforce. It's also an extremely effective marketing strategy. The degree to which parents believe in the educational value of screen media influences how much their children watch. One national survey found that of children whose parents believe television helps learning, 76 percent watch TV every day. Of children whose parents believe television hurts learning, only 48 percent watch daily.[9] Another survey found that more than 28 percent of parents cite the belief that screen media is educational as their number one reason for placing their babies in front of it and 20 percent cite its value as a babysitter while they get things done around the house.[10]

For overstressed, overworked parents, it would be a godsend if babies really did benefit from the myriad videos and computer programs claiming to educate them. The problem is that they don't. There is no credible evidence that screen media is educational or beneficial in any way for babies and toddlers.[11] Everything we know about how our youngest children learn points away from screens to what they do naturally— engage with the people who love them best and explore the world around them with all five of their senses. Meanwhile, research suggests that that the more time babies spend with screen media, the less time they spend in those two essential activities. A study of how children ages three to five use their time found that for every hour of television watched, they spend forty-five minutes less in creative play. Babies and toddlers lose even more time than their older brothers and sisters—fifty-two minutes for every hour of TV.[12]

Psychologist Jean Piaget called the first years of life the "sensory-motor" stage of development because that's how babies learn—through touch and the rest of their senses. Once they can crawl or walk, the imperative to move is irresistible and the arena for exploration expands. In contrast to their older brothers and sisters, they aren't yet able to use language and symbolic thought as tools for sorting out their environment.

Envision eating dinner with three-year-old Max and Anna, his twelve-month-old sister. Max sits in a booster seat. His plate and silverware may be plastic, his cup may have a lid, and his parents still cut his food, but he has enough self-control to be at the table for some amount of time without wreaking havoc. Anna sits on her father's lap. She may have a spoon to bang, a cracker to munch with newly emerged front teeth, and other little bits of food that eventually end up in her mouth. Sometimes she and her dad make funny noises at each other. Her place at the table is notable for the wide empty space around her. Plates, cup, glasses, bowls, and utensils have been pushed as far away as possible so that Anna's dad can still eat, but she can't reach them. Max may not like to sit still for long periods of time, but no one worries that he's going to stab himself or anyone else with a fork. It's safe for him to be near the salad bowl. As Anna strains to reach the salt shaker and chews on her spoon, Max asks questions. Why is lettuce green? Where did Grandpa's hair go? What's inside my skin?

We push plates and cups away from a twelve-month-old because, as babies grow, their reach exceeds both their judgment and their self-control. That's why, when they begin to move, we baby-proof whole rooms and houses for their own protection and to keep fragile family treasures safe as well. To maximize toddlers' freedom to explore, we remove breakable, potentially dangerous objects and replace them with ones that can be handled, chewed on, and dropped repeatedly.

A toddler's natural imperative to explore through movement, touch, and taste can be an exciting and exhausting time for parents. Eventually, as children begin to gain the capacity to associate mental images with actual objects and actions—and to use language to express their needs and desires—they begin to gain some satisfaction from thinking about something rather than from doing it. They also become better able to resist their impulses both to move and to handle everything in sight. Their need to explore becomes a habit of mind and, once they outgrow babyhood, they can satisfy some of their curiosity mentally or verbally. They maintain their need to explore, but grabbing gives way to questions; they can anticipate the consequences of actions such as touching a hot stove.

What if Anna's hand was slapped when she knocked over her father's glass of water or tried to grab his mashed potatoes?

What would happen if most of Max's questions went unanswered or he was ridiculed for wondering? Suppose his environment was so filled with electronic distractions that he didn't have time or space to even formulate questions.

With socialization and growing self-control, Anna will learn not to grab. With a growing mastery of language and symbolic thought, she too will ask questions. Eventually, if they are allowed to continue their playful exploration of the world, both children will have the skills to answer some of their questions by thinking them through. They will expand their tools for satisfying their curiosity beyond questions to active exploration. What they are curious about and how they satisfy that curiosity will vary, depending on their own interests and predilections.

In the spring of 2007, an internationally renowned group of researchers in early learning issued a statement about children and learning based on the available scientific evidence. They stated that children are active, not passive, learners who acquire knowledge by examining and exploring their environment.[13] They gain the skills essential to active learning through play. For very young children, play and active learning are indistinguishable.

One consequence of putting infants in front of screens is that TV viewing seems to be habituating. The more television babies and toddlers watch, the more they watch when they get older.[14] Research and common sense tell us that if we allow screen media to play a big part in the lives of children under two they are going to want to engage with screens even more as they get older. Babies used to depending on screen media to alleviate boredom or to calm down are going to continue to need it as they grow. As every parent knows, it's harder to take a privilege or activity away from children once it's established than it is to increase privileges incrementally. "But, Dad," the argument is likely to go, "you let me watch TV all the time when I was little. Why can't I watch it now?"

For parents immersed in the often bewildering and all-encompassing experience of raising young children, it's hard to anticipate how our decisions today are going to affect our family life several years in the future. But given the proliferation of electronic media and a marketing industry spending nearly $17 billion annually to target kids,[15] struggles about screens can foment family stress until children leave home.

In addition to taking babies away from play, television viewing for children under the age of three is also linked to doing less well on math and reading tests at the age of six—regardless of how much TV the children watch over the age of three.[16] Researchers have found a link between infant television viewing and irregular sleep patterns, which can interfere with learning.[17] A preschooler's risk for obesity increases by 6 percent for every hour of TV watched per day. If there's a TV in the child's bedroom, the odds jump an additional 31 percent for every hour watched.[18] Obesity rates are highest among children who watch four or more hours of television a day and lowest among children who watch an hour or less a day.[19] For children three and under, other studies suggest that the more TV they watch, the more likely they are—when they become grade school students—to score lower on IQ and academic tests and engage in bullying behavior.[20]

It is horrible when children's lives are blighted by disaster—by hunger, poverty, illness, abuse, or war. But it seems both strange and sad that our society deprives even infants who aren't hungry, or homeless, or victimized by tragedy the opportunity to grow and develop the skills and habits essential for leading meaningful, creative lives. Yet, in spite of a risk-benefit ratio suggesting that it would be prudent to keep our youngest and most vulnerable children away from screens, "edutainment" for babies, where commercial culture meets electronic wizardry and pedagogical jargon, is booming.

In *Consuming Kids*, I credit the success of the baby video industry to *Teletubbies*, the first-ever television program for babies, which the Public Broadcasting System imported from Britain in 1998—and marketed with all sorts of unsupported claims. Among its other alleged virtues, *Teletubbies* was supposed to facilitate infant language development, teach babies how to play, and help children get comfortable with technology.[21] What *Teletubbies* proved is that deceptive marketing can be lucrative. By 2007, the series and its licensed toys, clothing, and paraphernalia for babies and toddlers generated over $1 billion in sales around the world.[22] Its financial success sealed the media fate of infants and toddlers in the United States.

In 2001, Disney acquired its own media property for babies—*Baby Einstein*, a video series purporting to be educational even for newborns.[23] Five years later, betting on the brand loyalty cemented by parents' devotion to Baby Einstein, Disney executives created *Little Einsteins*, a program for preschoolers that now appears on the Disney Channel. With the Disney marketing machine behind it, and a host of licensed toys, the brand is booming. Disney executives claim that two out of three mothers in the United States have purchased a Baby Einstein product. The brand brought in $200 million in 2005 and Disney expects it to generate $1 billion annually by 2010.[24]

Everything about Baby Einstein's marketing strategy—from the brand's name to the company's slogan "Great minds start little" to the titles of individual videos, such as *Baby Wordsworth: First Words Around the House*; *Baby Galileo: Discovering the Sky*; *Numbers Nursery*; *Baby Da Vinci: From Head to Toe*—

sends a message to parents that its contents are educational. Some DVD boxes even have a sticker on the front that says "Bonus Learning!"

Baby Wordsworth is marketed as fostering language development. *Baby Galileo* is supposed to introduce babies to the night sky. *Numbers Nursery* claims to introduce babies to numbers. *Baby Da Vinci* "presents [babies] with a playful and interactive introduction to the human body in three languages"[25] Never mind that that television has proven to be a poor tool for helping babies learn words;[26] that they learn the meaning of numbers by handling blocks, or carrots, or crackers; or that they identify body parts by exploring their own bodies. As for learning French or Spanish, television has not been found to be an effective tool for teaching babies foreign languages.[27] And a recent study from the University of Washington suggests that for babies between the ages of eight and sixteen months, watching baby videos may even negatively affect word acquisition.[28]

Steveanne Auerbach, known as Dr. Toy, and a veteran observer of toy industry trends, sees the arrival of the Leapfrog company, founded in 1995, as the beginning of the edutainment industry as we know it today.[29] Leapfrog, which specializes in merging portable computer gaming technology with the star quality of licensed media characters to create so-called educational computer games for children, originally aimed its products at four- to eight-year-olds. By 2003, the company was targeting babies.[30] It's now the third largest toy company in the United States, threatening toy giants Mattel and Hasbro, who are now developing and marketing "edutainment" of their own.[31]

Leapfrog manufactures one of the more worrisome "educational" products for infants on the market—the "Magic Moments" Learning Seat, advertised as suitable for newborns.[32] It looks like a typical baby seat—padded, with straps to secure the baby, who is not actually seated but is lying down comfortably at about a 45-degree angle. What sets Magic Moments apart is that directly in the baby's line of vision—partially obstructing her view of the world and therefore limiting, rather than enhancing, possibilities for learning—is a mirror that turns into a screen every time she moves. The Seat is described this way:

> With an ultra-cozy seat, wide base and magic mirror activity bar, baby will create magical learning moments. For every tap of an animal, the magic mirror reveals colorful images, and baby is introduced to learning songs, words and classical music that promote early language and future reading development, while encouraging gross motor skill development and tactile exploration! Baby can also kick to bring the songs, music and lights to life! Three modes allow parent to level the learning experience and stimulate baby with more play options. Additional features include, a Gentle Touch™ vibration system that delivers three soothing wave-like vibrations to help relax baby.[33]

One of the arguments parents make for placing screens in front of babies is that the babies stare at them so intently that parents are convinced the experience of watching must be meaningful. However, pediatrician Dimitri Christakis, who researches the impact of media on babies, pointed out the following when interviewed on NPR's *All Things Considered*: "[Screen media] directed at young infants exploit[s] the orienting reflex. By constantly changing themes, having flashing lights and sound, they keep the child focused on the screen. They have to do that, in effect, because infants don't understand the content, right? They don't actually know what they're looking at. They're stimulated by the constant changing scenery."[34] The fact that Leapfrog has figured out a way to interpose a screen between a baby and the rest of the world is chilling—and so is its marketing. The Learning Seat's screen is described as the source of babies' "magical learning moments," implying that it, not the world around them, is a source of wonder and educational opportunities.

Meanwhile, the objects dangling in front of the baby are not there to be explored and investigated in and of themselves. Their only value is that they activate the screen. When the lion moves, an abstract yellow sun flashes on the screen and a disembodied voice can be heard saying things like "Yellow lion," "Large lion," "Touch my mane," and "Lion roars at the sun." Phrases like these seem to be the basis for Leapfrog advertising suggesting that the seat promotes early language development and literacy. Given that the lion never changes size, there's no explanation of what a mane is, or even the whisper of a roar, it's hard to see how any of those phrases—provided with no context—would be educational for even an older child. In any case, research suggests that screen media is not an effective means of teaching new vocabulary to toddlers, who acquire language best from live human voices.[35]

Baby toys that work mechanically rather than through computer technology are now dismissed as old-fashioned; yet these toys promote eye-hand coordination by encouraging pulling, turning, twisting, and spinning as well as pushing. A baby ensconced in the Magic Moments Learning Seat merely has to bat at something to get a spectacular effect. Play, and the satisfactions gained from it, requires effort. If all babies ever have to do is bat at an object or press a button, they miss opportunities for learning how to explore and create. A colleague recently told me about giving her twenty-two-month-old granddaughter a stuffed bear. "She kept squeezing its hands and punching its stomach," she said, "and finally I realized—she was trying to make it do something!"

The seat comes with a guide suggesting ways that parents can interact with the babies ensconced in its cushions. Yet clearly, with its jiggling motion and the self-generated screen images and noise, the Magic Moments Learning Seat is designed to occupy babies without their parents' interactions. Like many edutainment products, including Baby Einstein videos, which have a repeat-play option,[36] parents get a double message. On the one hand, the products may be sold with suggestions for interacting with babies. On the other hand, they are created with all sorts of features that remove parents from the necessity of engaging.

When I was at dinner in a favorite restaurant the other night, I watched two families—each consisting of two parents and a toddler—cope very differently with the challenges of eating out with children ensconced in that stage of development where their delight in active exploration supersedes their delight in anything else, including eating.

One family came equipped with a bright red portable DVD player. Their son was immersed in *Thomas the Tank Engine,* a highly regarded television program for preschoolers, throughout their meal. He was completely silent and oblivious to his surroundings, absentmindedly chewing on the morsels of food his mom fed him from her fork. His parents were able to enjoy their meal uninterrupted. They were even able to carry on an extended conversation, an admittedly rare experience for parents of very young children.

The other parents had a less peaceful meal. After their toddler reached the limit of his tolerance for being confined in a high chair, rather than distracting him from the urge to explore the sights and sounds of the restaurant, his parents took turns walking him around. Clutching a plastic spoon, he spent several minutes with his nose pressed against a case of fancifully decorated pastries. He made shoveling gestures with his spoon and held it up to his mom. "Are you giving me a taste?" she asked. "Yum!" Laughing, he did it again. "Up" he said, pointing to the top row of cakes. "That's right," his mom said. "The pink cakes are up." "Down!" he chortled, bending his knees a little as he pointed to the bottom row. Holding his mom's hand, he trotted back to their table where he was handed over to his dad, ending up back at the pastry case while his mom finished her dinner. With his parents' help, his inborn capacity for playful exploration transformed the restaurant into a laboratory for exploring color, spatial concepts, and make believe.

What about the little boy with his own portable DVD player? I saw a similar model advertised on television a while ago in a commercial showing a clip from Nickelodeon's highly regarded *Blue's Clues* and ending with the tag line "Watch this educational program." *Thomas the Tank Engine* is marketed as promoting imagination. "With Thomas & Friends," the official Web site says, "children enter a world of imagination through the tracks of a train and the words of a story. As children embark for fun with their engine friends, adventures unfold that lead to timeless life lessons. Parents and children enjoy a unique connection on every journey."[37]

It's certainly possible that a preschooler whose only screen experience each day was one episode of *Thomas* could be inspired to play creatively about it. But, as we know, children of all ages are consuming significantly more than thirty minutes a day of screen media. Thanks to the miracles of modern technology and aggressive marketing campaigns, programming such as *Thomas and Friends, Dora the Explorer*, and *Arthur* accompany children out to dinner, ride with them to school in the backseat of cars, and follow them across the country on plane trips. As a senior vice president at Nickelodeon explained, "There's a lot of evidence that kids are using [media content on] cell phones to be entertained in the interstitial parts of their lives, and we decided to start with something that will involve the parents."[38] But as the media and marketing industries are pushing children to embrace a life of all screens all the time, we need to ask ourselves some questions about the educational value of electronic media that go beyond concerns about media content.

What are the primary life lessons children absorb by regularly watching DVDs while eating in a restaurant? They learn to look to screens rather than to their environment for stimulation, to expect to be entertained rather than to entertain themselves. They learn that interacting with family during meals is so boring that they need the inducement of screen entertainment to get through a meal. And they learn that eating is something to do while you're doing something else.

What about the lessons children don't learn when they are glued to a screen even as they are out and about? They miss feeling those unsettling niggles of curiosity that lead to the delights of active exploration, and they miss the exhilarating sense of mastery and pride that comes with discovery and problem solving. They lose out on chances to nurture and preserve their innate sense of wonder. They miss opportunities to practice delaying gratification, which is essential for any task that involves setting a goal and working toward it, from succeeding at work to saving for retirement. They don't learn to discover what's unique about them in the world—what piques their interest enough that they will become passionate about it. They miss opportunities to play in and with their surroundings in their own unique ways.

At a major department store, waiting outside a dressing room while my daughter tried on some clothes, I watched a girl of about eight wait for her mom. The store had placed television sets overhead by all the changing areas to amuse (and advertise to) people waiting for someone trying on clothes. This particular TV was broken. The girl sat on a bench kicking her heels in rhythm. As time went on, she stood up and began jumping around the floor, which was covered in alternating black and white squares of linoleum. It became clear that she had invented a kind of hopscotch that involved landing only in black squares. She seemed perfectly content. I suspect that if the screen had worked she would have been watching it. Have you noticed how hard it is to ignore a screen when we're in its presence? It's a protective instinct for our eyes to be drawn to light and rapid movement. Because the screen was broken, however, she had to do what kids waiting for their moms to try on clothes did until just a few years ago: she had to fall back on her own resources for entertainment. She was able to take charge of her environment, exercising both her body and her mind as she waited.

A magazine ad for the Chevy Venture minivan—one of the first cars to promote screens in the backseat—shows a little boy totally mesmerized, staring up at a screen. The tagline, reeking with cynicism and irony, reads: "Videos: they're definitely changing the way kids behave these days," and adds below, "So everyone can enjoy the ride." The marketing industry spends billions of dollars targeting children with messages of "empowerment," which induces children to nag their parents and think of adults as nitwits worthy only of disrespect.[39] At the same time, they market sedation to adults as a means of coping with the bratty behavior they're encouraging. The subtext of the Venture ad is, "Stick children in front of a screen to subdue them: they're a pain in the ass."

Resisting ubiquitous, brilliantly crafted marketing campaigns is hard enough for the overstressed parents of babies and toddlers, especially when those campaigns simultaneously play into their worst fears (their children won't succeed in school) and offer them a guilt-free and much needed respite (an electronic babysitter that is actually good for kids). The marketing industry's false claims that screen media is beneficial for babies becomes even harder to dispel when organizations whose reputations are built on their dedication to the well-being of children start luring babies to screens. Once Disney began targeting babies in an effort to inculcate lifetime loyalty to the Disney brand, Sesame Workshop, the venerated producers of *Sesame Street*, jumped into the market as well by partnering with Zero to Three, an equally venerated public health organization, to create videos for infants and toddlers. Even aside from its competition with Disney, it's not surprising that Sesame Workshop wanted to get into baby video marketing. One thing that babies *do* learn from videos is to become familiar with the characters they're watching and to enjoy recognizing them.[40] Sesame Workshop earned $46.8 million in licensing fees in 2006—it's a major source of support. The company created a whole new line of licensed products to go with the new videos.[41]

There were at least 750 baby videos on the market in 2006, and they continue to multiply like rabbits.[42] Michael Eisner, former head of Disney, bought Team Baby, a company producing videos designed to brand babies with college sports teams.[43] BabyPro, another company, claims that "watching these videos will encourage your baby to kick, throw, swim, dance, surf, dance and cheer—for a lifetime!"[44] On the research section of its Web site—and citing no research except for the debunked and misunderstood "Mozart effect," beloved by most baby video companies*—BabyPro proclaims that its product promotes "self-confidence, builds skill depth and provides a foundation for a lifetime of healthy, active sports play!"[45]

Nor are the major religions to be left behind. Christians can avail themselves of *Praise Baby* videos to promote the trappings of Christianity to their infants, while Jews can turn to *Oy Baby* 1 and 2, and those Buddhists who are so inclined can make use of *Zen Baby*—and spend less time with their babies inculcating the basic spiritual tenets of love, compassion, empathy, and an appreciation for the ineffable splendors of life, qualities that develop over time through interaction with caring adults. I've yet to see a Muslim baby video, but that doesn't mean it isn't out there.

The allure of screen time as a quick fix for parental stress, in combination with educational policies as well as the other forces in society that deprive children of time and space to play—overscheduling, lack of outdoor play space, lack of adequate day care—constitute an assault on children's creative playtime so powerful that it is tempting to throw up our hands in despair and make a baby video series—*Baby Robot,* we could call it, featuring individual titles like *Baby Blobby*, *Baby Blasé*, and *Baby Boredom*.

---

*Many of the baby videos I've looked at cite research that listening to classical music is linked to infant intellectual development. There has never been research showing this to be the case. In 1993 Frances H. Rauscher et al. published a study entitled "Music and Spatial Task Performance," which suggested that college students who listened to Mozart before taking the Stanford-Binet IQ test did better on spatial subtests. The study has never been replicated, but continues to be cited in baby video marketing.

But before we all cash in on the baby video market and turn our backs on play, I want to talk more about why we shouldn't throw in the towel—how and why creative play is essential to children's well-being, the extraordinary ways that the children I've known make use of make believe, and what we can do to preserve it.

True Romance

My Love Affair with D.W. Winnicott

I lost my heart to the British pediatrician and psychoanalyst D.W. Winnicott over twenty-five years ago and have remained true to him ever since. Never mind the fact that he was (1) already married and (2) no longer alive when we first became intimate. It's Winnicott who gave us the comforting notion of "good enough" parenting—the idea that parents don't have to be perfect to raise healthy happy children—and linked play to creativity and mental health.[1]

By 1974, when I entered graduate school, I was earning my living as a children's entertainer. I had a notion that I could use my puppets in some kind of ongoing way with kids, but I wasn't sure how. I'd spent a year with a Head Start program in Boston's South End, where, under the rubric of language development, I sat with my puppets and talked with four- and five-year-olds. What continued to astonish me was the intimacy of the revelations these children made to Audrey Duck—about their parents, for instance, or about going to the dentist, or about dying, or about anger. Over the same span of time, I began to reflect on the specific ways I used my own puppet play to cope with difficult life issues.

That spring I took a course in play and symbol development. The reading list was filled with erudite esoterica, most of which made no sense to me. Therefore it was with something like despair that I opened Winnicott's book *Playing and Reality*. An hour or so later, I emerged from the first five chapters utterly transformed but with absolutely no intellectual grasp of what I had just read.

What I did understand was that my experience of puppets and puppet play was both explainable and of potentially significant value to other people. Although at the time I couldn't really understand why, Winnicott gave me the push I needed to begin thinking about puppets and play in the context of psychological theory and practice. Acquiring a systematic understanding of how and why puppets work as therapeutic tools is essential to using them effectively as agents for growth and change, for making sense of the themes and content they evoke, and for making decisions about how to use them therapeutically across a wide range of situations.

I bought my own copy of *Playing and Reality*, which sat on my bookshelf for years, more as a talisman than anything else, and set about trying to become a puppet therapist.

After working at Boston Children's Hospital for several years doing play therapy with puppets, after years of clinical supervision, and after I returned to school to get a doctorate in psychology, I reread *Playing and Reality* and went on to read other books by Winnicott. By then I understood enough to see that my intuitive reaction to Winnicott made sense. His theories about play, health, and creativity were a validation of my own journey and created both a context for therapeutic puppetry and the roots of a philosophy for living. But I had to laugh when I read what one of his protégées wrote about him: "You can only understand Winnicott if you already know what he is talking about." That was certainly my experience.

What Winnicott talks about is play. Play as a manifestation of health. Play as healing. Play as a means of honest self-expression. Play as creativity. Play as . . . and as I'm writing this I find myself imagining a dialogue with my puppet Audrey Duck that goes something like this:

AUDREY: I'm standing by.

ME: What for?

AUDREY: You're going to need me for all this theory stuff.

ME (*annoyed*): It's not "stuff." It's an amazing way of understanding the links between play, creativity, and health. You know, I'd really like to try to explain it myself.

AUDREY: I am yourself. Trust me, I'm going to come in handy any paragraph now. Winnicott would have loved me. So why are we talking about this?

ME: I'm hoping that if people really understand the hows and whys of creative play, they'll understand how important it is.

AUDREY: And?

ME (*laughing apologetically—I am embarrassed by my earnestness*): And they'll ensure that children have time and space to play in ways that nurture imagination and creative thinking.

AUDREY: And?

ME: And they will stop bombarding children with prefabricated entertainment that requires only that they observe or react rather than actively engage.

AUDREY (*slyly*): Prefabricated entertainment like television? Or computer games? Or electronic toys?

ME: Uh-huh.

AUDREY: And?

ME: And they'll understand that creative play is a great way for children to express—and grapple with—hard or powerful or scary thoughts and feelings. And they'll also understand that even very young children can have passionate, powerful feelings.

AUDREY: And?

ME: And that the capacity to play—even for grown-ups—is essential to leading a meaningful life.

AUDREY: And?

ME (*still embarrassed—I'm feeling quite vulnerable*): And for society—for keeping democracy alive. The skills children acquire in creative play—like problem solving, cooperation, empathy, and divergent thinking—are essential for people living in a democracy.

AUDREY: And?

ME (*exhausted*): Isn't that enough?

AUDREY: It's enough for me. I hate just reacting. I like to think for myself! Be original! Create! Emote!

ME (*marveling*): You're really into this.

AUDREY: Into it? I *am* it!

While my thinking about make believe and its links to health, not just for individuals but for society, is deeply rooted in my understanding of Winnicott and his theories, it has been influenced significantly by many of the giants of twentieth-century psychological theory. The links between fantasy and inner life are first found in the works of Sigmund Freud, as is the notion of play as a means of psychological mastery—or gaining a sense of control—over seemingly overwhelming events. His daughter, Anna Freud, explored the use of play as a means of helping children work through trauma. Jean Piaget also wrote about mastery, but he talks about it from a cognitive perspective. Psychologist Erik Erikson, although he was writing primarily about block play, put forth the idea that a central conflict or theme is inherent in every child's play construction and that the theme reflects the child's current developmental challenge. I've included suggested reading at the back of this book for anyone interested in exploring these and other sources for themselves. However, much of my current thinking about how and why make believe is important is also based on my own years of experience as a therapist, as a children's entertainer, and as someone who has, since childhood, delighted in the paradoxical experience of finding myself by getting lost in a particular kind of play—speaking to and through puppets.

A long time has passed since I first encountered Winnicott, and even more time has passed since he was writing and practicing. As in any long-term relationship, my initial blind infatuation transformed into something more real as I began to recognize the object of my affection's limitations as well as his strengths. Like all of us, Winnicott was limited by the times in which he lived. He was writing at a time when families were less likely to be seen in the context of a larger society, when mothers were almost always the primary child-care providers, and when "normal" was defined by the mores of middle- to upper-class white society. He did not take into account the fact that the children and families he saw were living in a larger society, nor did he take into account the terrible impact of poverty on children's health and well-being, nor did he acknowledge differing cultural norms in raising children. But those limitations notwithstanding, his theories are a gift to anyone raising children. He didn't believe that parents had to be perfect—only "good enough." And even now I believe Winnicott's thinking about play is central to an understanding of the phenomenon, its link to health and creativity, and the characteristics of environments that allow it to flourish.

> AUDREY: Wait! Wait! Wait!
>
> ME: What's the matter?
>
> AUDREY: Creativity. I'm tripping over "creativity." We can't all be artists. We're *not* all artists. *I'm* not. (*Loftily*) I don't think of myself as creative. I think of myself as created.
>
> ME: But I'm not just talking about creating art. I'm talking about creative living.
>
> AUDREY: "Creative living"? Sounds like an upscale furniture magazine.
>
> ME: I'm talking about creativity as the capacity to *generate*—to interact with life and make it meaningful. The capacity to imagine possibilities where none are obvious. To solve problems. To wrestle with new ideas and rethink old ones. To reflect on our experience and grow from it. That's what we do when we play.
>
> AUDREY: Oh. I get it. Living creatively.

A basic tenet of Winnicott's work is that play flourishes from infancy in the context of environments that are simultaneously secure enough to be safe and relaxed enough to enable spontaneous expression. The different possible ways we can hold and interact with babies provide a good metaphor for the impact of the environment on play. A baby held too loosely doesn't feel safe to generate movement and must remain perfectly still for fear of falling; a baby held too tightly has no space to generate movement and never has the experience of originating action. However, when babies are held securely enough to be safe and loosely enough to have some freedom of move-ment in the course of their development, they have the oppor-tunity to experience what it's like to generate action—to choose to make a gesture. Winnicott calls environments that are safe but allow for freedom of expression "holding" environments. It's a great term. A caretaker's arms can be a holding environment. So can a classroom. So can a relationship. So can a family.

Think about the different possible ways to respond to a baby. When a baby makes a gesture that seems purposeful, or that suggests independent personhood, we often respond—without even thinking about it—with a coo or a smile or a laugh. In that interchange are the seeds of two important de-velopmental changes essential to creativity.

By originating an action that evokes a distinct reaction from her environment, the baby begins to learn to differentiate her-self from her parent and to establish a sense of herself as a sep-arate being. The knowledge that we are different from our environment, and from the people around us, is an essential foundation for healthy growth and development. If, as babies, our early actions evoke loving responses from the important adults in our lives, we each experience our burgeoning self as able to make good things happen in the world. We experience creativity.

An *inadequate* holding environment may be one that is filled with failures that compromise safety, or it may be one that constantly bombards the baby with demands to react rather than initiate action. Suppose the baby makes a gesture and no one responds. Suppose she generates a gesture that elicits anger instead of support. Suppose people are so busy eliciting responses from her ("Do this!" "Smile!" "Do that!") that she has no space to even *try* to generate an action on her own. How does she ever learn who she really is?

Winnicott's writings imply that a child growing up in an environment that is either unsafe as the result of neglect or too demanding as the result of incessant stimulation and demands to respond may develop a reactive, or "false," self instead of the "true," or creative, self that flourishes in a supportive holding environment. Creativity, or constructive spontaneity, in contrast to the constant compliance or reactivity demanded by what Winnicott calls an "impinging" environment, is at the core of his conception of the difference between mental health and illness.

As children grow, their environment expands far beyond the safety of nestling in our arms. But their need for "holding" in order to play spontaneously and creatively continues both in their physical environments and in their relationships. They need to be both physically and emotionally safe. They need room to explore and experiment within boundaries that protect them from harm without constriction. They need physical space in the form of safe play areas, and they need adult relationships that simultaneously nurture freedom of expression and delineate clear boundaries that keep them from being either hurt or hurtful. They also need silence and time on their own in order to experience the difference between reacting to outside stimulation and generating their own ideas in play.

Play is often described as the "work" of children, to stress play's essential role in children's development and to convince an increasingly rigid, results-oriented adult society to value and promote its practice. It's a way of saying, "See—play looks like wasting time because it seems like so much fun. But, really, when kids play they are hard at work learning all sorts of skills." I was visiting a preschool recently and was surprised to see a series of signs up on the wall with phrases like, "When I play with water, I am learning about the physical world and the nature of materials." Each sign linked a particular kind of play (blocks, sand, dress-up) to the acquisition of specific skills. When I asked about the signs the preschool's director said that she put them up in response to parents who were nervous about the fact that their children were "just playing" all day. Strategically, to prevent the complete demise of play-based early-childhood education, we may have to refer to play as work, but in fact there are some important distinctions between the two.

Play can be a component of working. Often it's the part that we most enjoy—when we generate ideas and projects or solve problems. However, once meeting a goal, making a deadline, seeking approval, or earning a profit become of primary importance, the experience ceases to be play. The results of work are of paramount importance. But the *experience* of play, alone, is exquisitely satisfying. Play is an end in itself and, paradoxically, it's when we abandon ourselves to the process of playing that it contributes most to our growth and development.

Play implies movement (think of the "play" of a rope), action ("in play"), and drama ("playing" a role). Within a holding environment, play allows us to bring forth what Winnicott calls "dream potential." We can express our deepest wishes, hopes, fears, and fantasies without the risk of real-world consequences. We can actively experiment with our dreams (or nightmares) in a uniquely safe space. Over time we are able to use play to wrestle with life experiences that may seem incomprehensible or overwhelming and gain mastery over them. In doing so, we can integrate experience—and our feelings about that experience— into a cohesive, meaningful sense of ourselves and the world. Therapists call this experience "working through."

The need to gain a sense of mastery or competence in a complicated world is the motivation behind a core characteristic of children's play that many adults find frustrating: their delight in repetition. Children often use repetitive play to make sense of, and get a handle on, a life challenge that may seem overwhelming, confusing, or just plain interesting. "How many times can she play peek-a-boo?" groans the father of a six-month-old. The answer is probably "endlessly" or close to it. One person's peek-a-boo is another person's means of coming to grips with separation—of truly understanding that beloved people and familiar objects won't disappear forever when they are out of sight. "Jessica always wants to play the same thing, and I get so tired of it," sighs the mother of a two-and-a-half-year-old. "She's the mommy and I'm the child. She's dropping me off at day care, going to work, and returning to pick me up—over and over and over again." In a sense, Jessica's play is a more sophisticated game of peek-a-boo. The same principle applies: by creating a situation that allows her to be the one doing the leaving, Jessica gets a chance to gain mastery over the pain of being left and to reassure herself that these separations aren't forever. Sometimes children in the midst of grappling with a new element in their lives play out variations of the same theme for months at a time.

At almost three, Megan was a happy, well-adjusted little girl who digested the news that she was going to be a big sister in silence. After a long moment, she slid off the couch to find her favorite rubber baby doll. Grabbing its leg, she enthusiastically whomped it on the floor and hurled it across the room. Turning back to her rather stunned parents, she grinned and cheerfully announced, "No more baby!"

When I relayed this story to a friend with an admitted distaste for displays of strong emotion, he was horrified. The intensity of Megan's feelings scared him. "Supposing she does that to the real baby?" he asked. I wasn't worried.

It's a rare only child who greets news of a new baby in the family with unmixed joy. Megan's intense negative feelings about her impending sibling are not remarkable. Anger, grief, and fear of being displaced are common—and understandable—reactions, even in very young children. While I don't advocate encouraging kids to hurl their toys across the room, I see Megan's behavior as a sign of health. What fills me with awe is her capacity to use play to help her cope with—and communicate—her feelings at such an early age. No one told her to do it. Nor has Megan been in play therapy. She is, however, growing up in an environment that provides opportunities for her to play spontaneously. While her home isn't television-free, TV does not yet play a dominant role in her life. Megan's short life includes plenty of room for the tools and opportunities that engender pretend play. No one told her to play about her feelings, but she knew instinctively that she could. That she had strong feelings about the new baby is not surprising. What delights me and my child development colleagues is how clearly she chose to express those feelings.

In the ensuing months, Megan's parents were wise enough to provide her with endless opportunities to play out the new baby's arrival. She began to dress up in her mom's shoes and carry her baby doll everywhere. She tenderly fed the "baby," diapered it, and dropped it off at day care. One day she announced, "When I get frustrated [actually, having trouble with her r's, she said "fwustwated"] with the baby, I'm going to kick it." Her parents were able to play along with her, and in doing so they modeled tenderness and gentleness with her baby dolls. They were able to reassure her before the new baby arrived that everyone feels frustrated sometimes, but that we can't hurt people because of it. By allowing Megan to play about her feelings, fears, and fantasies about the new baby, they helped her develop coping skills for managing frustration.

As the infant in her mother's uterus developed, Megan's play about babies evolved. She literally stepped into her mother's shoes and stuffed doll after doll under her shirt, giving birth several times a day. She and her parents diapered her dolls and bathed them. In her own time, in her own way, and in a safe space, she wrestled with a host of cognitive and emotional issues raised by the new baby's impending arrival. What was it like to be pregnant? How did the baby get in there, anyway? What did it mean that she was no longer going to be an only child? How was she going to cope with sharing? Was it okay that she was sometimes angry about it? What could she do with her anger? When her baby sister was born, Megan greeted her with tenderness. She did not, as my friend feared, attack the baby. She continues to be—mostly—gentle with her little sister, although she is still sometimes rough with her baby dolls. Her play about birth and babies has diminished considerably. It's not that she doesn't still have some feelings of envy or anger. Sometimes she gets a little rough with her baby sister. But because she was able to work with those "negative" feelings through her play, they became manageable. They do not drive her behavior. She can continue to express them, when necessary, in her play. Because she had done so much playing about these themes before her sister's birth, she is also able to talk about how she feels with the adults who love her.

Suppose no one had encouraged Megan's play. Suppose the adults around her were too busy or stressed or depressed to pay attention. Suppose they were so horrified at her initial outburst that they punished her. Suppose they demanded only expressions of unqualified enthusiasm about the approaching changes in their family. She would certainly have continued to harbor feelings of envy and rage, but she would not have talked or played about them. She might have added feelings of shame to the burden of her already uncomfortable feelings about the baby. She might, beyond the new baby, have generalized her parents' negative response to her expression of feelings to mean that she should never, under any circumstances, acknowledge anger. On the surface, she might have continued to act like the sweet, smiling little angel that her parents expected her to be.

In other words, with no opportunity to express her true feelings, a child like Megan might develop what Winnicott calls a "false self." She might grow up to be an incessantly sweet, smiling adult who is actually sitting on a volcano of unexpressed anger. Don't we all know people like that: people who smile all the time but seem somehow brittle and false? People who deny feeling anger, grief, or fear, even when they are smack in the middle of situations that, in anyone else, would evoke those responses—incessantly cheerful people who never seem angry, but often act hurtfully toward other people.

Powerful feelings can be overwhelming for young children if they have no acceptable outlet for expressing them. It's important to learn self-control, but it's also important for children to learn to recognize, and have acceptable outlets for, the whole range of their feelings. By allowing her to play out her feelings, Megan's parents helped her learn to understand and experience the difference between feeling and action. When children create frustrating situations for Audrey Duck, I might make her respond by saying, "I'm angry. I'm so angry that I feel like hitting." When that happens, I can say to my puppet (and the children get to hear), "It's okay to be angry, but you can't hit [kick, punch, hurt] someone." Later in the conversation I can have Audrey say, "I'm so angry that I feel like hitting—but I'm not going to." I'll acknowledge her anger and praise her for her self-control. The children get to witness someone grappling successfully with impulse control. They also get to hear an adult acknowledging the validity of their feelings.

The capacity for play is innate and can be fostered from infancy in the context of nurturing relationships that allow children to move safely from the total dependence of infancy toward independence. What makes being a parent of babies maturing into toddlerhood so challenging is that we are coping with creatures who—in rapid succession, sometimes almost simultaneously—have conflicting needs to be attached to and separate from the adults they love.

To cope with these normal and conflicting needs for separation and attachment, babies often turn to an object that already exists in their world—a soft toy, a stuffed animal, or a blanket—over which they have total control.

This motley collection of blankets, bears, and other cuddlies that Winnicott calls "transitional objects" appears as a baby begins the transition from total dependence toward independence. They become crucial for comfort or for going to sleep at night. In fact, they sometimes seem to be even more important than actual parents because children cannot bear to be parted from them.

Transitional objects seem like nothing special to the outside world, but their owners invest them with special meaning. They provide their owner-creators with enormous comfort. You've heard the phrase "security blanket." On the one hand, it's only a blanket; on the other hand, this particular blanket helps a particular child feel safe and no other blanket can replace it. The baby doesn't create the blanket. But the baby does create the blanket's meaning. And what's interesting, when transitional objects flourish, in part it's because adult caretakers accept the importance of their significance to their young owners.

This phenomenon is so nearly universal that it turns up in popular culture. Perhaps the best-known example of a transitional object is the blanket that Linus carries everywhere in Charles Schultz's *Peanuts* cartoons. And, from the mid-1980s through the mid-1990s, cartoon artist Bill Watterson based his comic strip *Calvin and Hobbes* on the relationship between a little boy and a stuffed tiger from whom he cannot bear to be parted.

One of the characteristics of transitional objects is that other people recognize their importance to the children who created them but do not invest them with the same meaning. In the eyes of their respective families and friends, these precious possessions are simply a blanket or a stuffed animal. But to Linus and Calvin, they are friends, protectors, lifelines, occasionally enemies to be vanquished, and who knows what else. They live at the intersection of inner experience and outer reality and, paradoxically, belong to both. They are a source of great joy and can also wreak some havoc when they get inadvertently separated from their creators.

I was recently visiting my niece and her family in another state when she, pregnant with a soon-to-arrive baby, had to be rushed unexpectedly to the hospital. Her two very young daughters and I, not very well acquainted yet, were left on our own more abruptly than any of us, including their mom and dad, would have liked. We all did splendidly until bedtime. Sarah, the oldest at four, explained to me that her little sister, Emily, needed her blanket "DiDi" in order to sleep and that I had to find it. "No problem," I thought, always delighted to nurture such relationships, and I began to hunt. I looked high and low and, with growing panic, realized that DiDi was likely to remain missing. It was a long night. Emily, rising admirably to the occasion, lay in bed mostly in silence, but periodically I heard her murmuring mournfully, "DiDi . . . DiDi . . . DiDi." Sarah, a protective older sister, eyed me reproachfully, "Emily can't go to sleep without DiDi," she explained again, sadly. I alternated between sitting with them to provide what comfort I could and engaging in an intense search around the house. Finally, Emily fell asleep on her own. Her mom spent the night in the hospital, she and the as yet unborn baby turned out to be fine, and Emily's dad returned in time to rescue DiDi from some nook or cranny I missed in my searches. DiDi was safe in bed with Emily when she woke the next morning.

I've heard concern from colleagues who work with parents and toddlers that they are observing fewer transitional objects in the lives of children. They speculate that parents may be too stressed to remember to validate the relationship, that screens are taking the place of comforting objects, and that even the public health dictum to place babies up to twelve months in cribs without stuffed animals may be contributing to their demise. There's no research about this and I hope it's not the case.

Winnicott believed that, while transitional objects fade in importance as children grow, the psychological space they occupy remains and that it's in that space that creative play takes place. Our childhood experience of what Winnicott calls "transitional space" as children affords us access as adults to a rich panoply of experiences that are neither wholly internal nor wholly external, but somehow both. Religious and patriotic symbols, like a cross, a Star of David, or a flag, for instance, have meaning beyond their physical properties that vary depending on your experience. Many types of psychotherapy occur at the intersection of real and not real, or inner and outer reality. Your interactions with a therapist, for instance, are real in that they actually happen, but they are a different kind of reality from that which holds sway in the rest of your life. A therapist's response to your expressed emotions, such as anger, is usually markedly different from the reactions of your friends and family. Visual art is another example of the paradox of straddling inner and outer reality, or of real and not real. A picture of a vase of flowers is real in that it exists in time and space, but the vase in the picture is also not real in that it isn't actually the object it represents. Together, the artist and the viewer "create" the symbolic vase: the artist makes an image and imbues it with his or her meaning; the viewer adds another level of meaning rooted in his or her own experience.

As children grow and develop, these stuffed animals and blankets become less and less important to their creators, and eventually they are placed in a drawer and cease to be a part of day-to-day living. But at that point something very wonderful happens. What remains, for the rest of our lives, is the capacity to experience a kind of psychological space that is simultaneously internal and external, real and not real, me and not me— a transitional space. In that space, once occupied by beloved transitional objects, people continue to assign personal, powerful meaning to objects from the outer world and to mold and shape these objects to give tangible shape to dreams, ideas, and fantasies. In other words, creative play becomes possible, and in playing we can truly be ourselves.

AUDREY: So what does playing have to do with me?
ME: It's interesting. Puppets exist in transitional space, and when they are used in play they instantly become like Win-

nicott's holding environment. Most people seem to experience puppets as a safe way to express thoughts or feelings they might not otherwise express. It's practically instantaneous.

AUDREY: And are puppets safe?

ME: Yes, most of the time. As long as no one forces people to make connections between their own feelings and their puppet play before they're ready to do that.

AUDREY: And am I your true self?

ME: You're certainly a part of it.

Of course false selves are probably necessary for living in society. "Company manners," for instance, are a kind of false-self phenomenon. But they can be maintained even as we recognize and have access to who we really are. By allowing children time and space for imaginative play we afford them an opportunity to experience their most creative "true" selves.

In play, not unlike artists, we express real feelings by using ideas or objects that are symbols for real objects. For instance, instead of throttling a real baby, Megan used a baby doll who could serve as a symbol of the new baby to express her anger. The creation of art through any medium is born in play, evolving from a space and circumstance that allow us to use that which the material world offers to express our own, unique, inner experience. To quote Winnicott one last time, we play "in the service of a dream."[2]

Because they are rooted in play, all art forms are powerful tools for self-expression. I find puppets to be particularly powerful. People talking through a puppet seem to feel shielded from exposure, and without even thinking about it they often use a puppet persona to express thoughts or feelings they might not otherwise divulge. This happens practically instantaneously with both adults and children, and in that sense puppets can function like Winnicott's holding environment. They provide a safe space for make believe that is simultaneously real and not real, internal and external.

Years ago when I was giving a workshop on creative puppet play with a group of teachers in New Hampshire, I noticed that one of them made a puppet whom she identified as a bank robber. To help the teachers practice using puppets I had each teacher engage in spontaneous dialogues with the puppet he or she made, talking about anything they chose. Each time the teacher with the bank robber puppet took her turn, she made her puppet urge her to rob a bank—a request that she, speaking as herself, resisted. As we went around the room one last time she created the following dialogue:

> BANK ROBBER: Come on. Rob a bank. It'll be easy.
> TEACHER: No it won't. I'll get caught. Look at Susan Saxe.
> BANK ROBBER: Aw, she was stupid.
> TEACHER: She wasn't. She got an A on that French test and I only got a B−.

The day before our workshop, Susan Saxe, a student from Brandeis University who participated in a bank robbery that was characterized as a political act, had been captured after several years of being underground. The teacher had been in school with her and therefore had a deeply personal connection to the story. She said afterward that she had no conscious idea about why she made a bank robber puppet, or even that Susan Saxe's capture was troubling her, until that exchange popped out of her mouth. It's certainly not a topic she would have raised in a room full of strangers, but it emerged as a central theme in the safety of her spontaneous, creative play.

Such instances are not unusual. At a recent workshop with a group of child-care administrators, I asked participants to make up a sentence that might be attributed to each of five puppets I showed them, one at a time. The room was somewhat stuffy and it was the middle of the afternoon during a very long day. One of the first lines offered in response to the first puppet I presented was, "I need a nap!" Everyone laughed, including the woman who said it. She realized instantly that she was talking about herself.

My years of experience exploring puppets as therapeutic tools are an essential component of my enormous respect for the deeply personal nature of creative play and its potential for helping us understand ourselves and cope with life's challenges. For that reason, I am going to share in-depth stories of some of the children with whom I've worked who used play therapy to sort through a variety of issues and concerns. I've included these stories to illustrate the intricacy and depth of children's psychological relationship to the play they create and as an argument for ensuring that we provide children with opportunities for make believe. As a therapist, my job is to work with children who for one reason or another need extra help coping with their lives. Most children don't need play therapy, but the relationship between our creative play and life experience exists even when children play on their own and the experience of playing has psychological benefit in and of itself. These stories, which include some discussion of how the themes and content of children's play influence my decisions as a therapist, are not meant to be taken as a how-to manual for play therapy, but rather as windows into experiencing the power of play as a means of self-expression and a tool for psychological health.

The children described in the next chapters are ordinary kids. With one exception—Michael—they happen to be coping with extraordinarily troubling circumstances. All of them are growing up in loving families with limited resources, and most of their families are coping with terrible stress. Yet each brings an awe-inspiring depth of feeling and perceptiveness to his or her make believe. Their play is simultaneously unique to them and universal in its reflection of the human condition. All of them engaged freely in our shared make believe. They were all free to stop pretending at any time, and sometimes they did for a short period of time, only to begin again. Each chose to use make believe to bring forth and explore deeply personal and sometimes terrifying thoughts and feelings about their lives. Nonetheless, there was an unmistakable element of joy and release in each of their creations.

I have selected these stories because each illustrates an important facet of allowing children to play—the ways that playing with children allows us to provide them with real-world models for coping, the need for boundaries, the ways that make believe allows us to truly be ourselves, and the ways that a child's play can educate us about the impact of our behavior and values on his or her life.

At first you might see the children I write about as completely different from the children you know and love—in part because what some of them are experiencing may seem so extreme. But they're not. In essence, these are children like any others, using play to cope with the challenges life has thrown them. Tragedies great and small invade even the most protected of childhoods. All children deserve a chance to develop their inner resources in order to master whatever challenges they face.

My relationship to these particular children is that of a therapist to a client. I've also played with children as a caretaker and teacher. In those roles, I let children's play unfold without probing, or even much guidance, although I may use puppets as a model for talking about feelings, or play as a means of introducing a difficult topic. As a performer I've often used puppets to create stories designed to help children think about challenging issues or cope with problems ranging from racism to abuse.

Puppetry is a powerful and underused medium for pretend play, but it is by no means the only one: doll play, drawing, sand play, block play, and telling stories (to name a few) are all excellent conduits for self-exploration and self-expression. My aim is not to persuade you that you should do the same things with children that I do, but to use these stories as an argument for respecting all children as the complex, deeply feeling people they are; for celebrating pretend play as an invaluable inborn resource; and for taking action to do what you can to provide children with the environments and relationships that enable make believe to flourish.

PART TWO

Make Believe and Making Meaning

Playing to Cope

5

Michael

Grappling with Change

Nineteen sixty-seven was a tough year to break into vaudeville, which had been dead for three decades. But I wasn't going to let that stop me. Buoyed by the unquenchable optimism and breathtaking disregard for reality that characterize the young, I dropped out of college and billed myself as Suzi Linn, the socially conscious ventriloquist.

Three stops on the subway transported me to the corner of Boylston and Tremont Streets, where the ghosts of vaudeville still lingered in Boston, across from an ancient, dilapidated graveyard housing the remains of Mother Goose. Each week I dutifully and hopefully visited the offices of Adams & Soper and James T. Kennedy, booking agents for magicians, singers, and comedians, along with a collection of various and sundry exotic dancers.

It was James T. and his sister, whose name was not on the door, who gave me my first job. I was to spend three weeks traveling with a troupe of performers in the Jordan Marsh Christmas Caravan. In the run-up to Christmas, we were that department store's gift to the poor and needy children of Boston and surrounding communities. I was launched!

The show was a winner. We opened with a Dixieland banjo player named Pat, sporting a straw hat, spiffy red jacket, and striped pants. Then Audrey Duck and I tripped lightly onto the stage, wowing our audiences with a magic trick featuring a collapsible flower. We were followed by Sammy Lyman, Stripe-O the Clown (whose career highlight was a Stripe toothpaste commercial) and his balloon creations, after which Ruth Tingley Seabury sang rousing renditions of Christmas carols, accompanying herself on her rhinestone-studded accordion. At the end of the show, Pat, who had been nipping at something backstage, staggered out as Santa Claus to distribute presents.

The shows themselves have coalesced in my memory into one glittering event. It's the life in between and some audience members that stick with me. We drove for hours on end, me in the backseat battling car sickness from the unbeatable aromatic combination of smoke from Sammy Lyman's cigarettes and the Old Spice aftershave that our Santa Claus doused himself with after his liquid lunches. The acrid smell of tuna fish and slightly old mayonnaise takes me instantly to the cafeterias of two or three Massachusetts homes for what were then called "the retarded." One indelible image is of a ward at Boston City Hospital and a little boy who was dying of leukemia—which at that time was not remotely curable. His eyes were blackened as if someone had punched him and his manner was listless, and all through my performance I kept feeling that dropping in for an hour's entertainment was a rather inadequate gesture.

I avoided Pat, but I got to know Sammy Lyman and Ruth Tingley Seabury pretty well. Sammy took me to Revere Beach—then a honky-tonk town north of Boston—to meet his girlfriend, a twenty-three-year-old ex-stripper named Felicia Vale.

A bleeding ulcer had put a stop to her career. In a tiny kitchen somewhere near the ocean, she cooked us fried matzoh, while generously passing on advice and some relics of her professional life. "You can always make a living dancing," she said cheerfully. Obviously, she didn't know me.

Midway through the tour, Ruth took me out to lunch at the Charlestown Navy Yard (her late husband was a navy man). She and her sister had led the kind of theatrical life I longed for—in their case playing accordion and singing together on the circuit, dressed in colonial costumes and white powdered wigs. Perched above Boston Harbor, surrounded by military decorum, she leaned forward earnestly over her iceberg lettuce with thousand island dressing. Even her perfectly made-up face could not mask her sincerity. "Never marry a man in show business, Susan," she told me that day. "They will do you dirt!"

The Jordan Marsh Christmas Caravan was the height of my vaudeville career, and it lasted a few weeks longer than my career as a nightclub performer, which began and ended with a performance at Jacques, a rather sketchy bar in the heart of Boston's abbreviated theater district.

At this point it was dawning on me that I wasn't cut out for show biz in the traditional sense. I couldn't escape my familial roots in social responsibility, which left me wanting to "do something useful." At the same time, I was determined to make my puppets the center of whatever doing something useful entailed. Certainly my experience visiting state institutions and hospitals that Christmas season was a factor in my decision to create a job as a puppet therapist at Children's Hospital nearly a decade later.

About a year after I gave up on vaudeville and was bumbling around trying to find a path for myself and my puppets, *Mister Rogers' Neighborhood* made its national debut. The program was astonishing in the way that it used puppets and fantasy to talk about really important issues for children. The entire program was a lesson in child development, but it was the segments in the Neighborhood of Make Believe that interested me the most. Fred Rogers was consciously using television, and puppet play, to help preschool children cope with fears, fantasies, and developmental challenges ranging from anxieties about going down the bathroom drain to worries about having a new baby in the family.

Inspired and intrigued, I wrote to Fred Rogers, who agreed to meet with me, a nineteen-year-old with few credentials, and I flew to Pittsburgh to begin what became a profoundly important relationship that lasted until his death in 2003. I appeared on his program periodically and worked with his production company to create video programs to help children cope with such difficult topics as having a mentally ill parent or returning to school after having been treated for cancer. Perhaps our most challenging work was a nine-episode series designed to help first- to third-graders grapple with racism, prejudice, and diversity.

These videos were based on research showing that live and televised stories, including those acted out with puppets, are a good way of encouraging pro-social behavior—what in psychological terms is called "modeling." Presentations featuring puppets or fantasy characters that are explicitly designed to promote pro-social behavior do have an impact on children's behavior, especially when the lessons in the stories are reinforced by discussions or activities related to the stories afterward.[1]

In my previous book, *Consuming Kids*, I relate an experience that was pivotal to my understanding of how puppets, theater, and the media can work as behavioral influencers. Early on in my performing career, I decided to include something about name-calling in one of my live performance pieces. I was going to have my puppet Audrey Duck call another puppet named Cat-a-lion "stupid," and then spend some time dealing with the ramifications—Cat-a-lion's hurt feelings and Audrey's sense of shame and guilt. The piece started out well enough. Audrey called Cat-a-lion "stupid" in her best taunting voice. She repeated it several times. The children were riveted. But then I heard a little voice from the audience calling out "Stupid!" Then another voice joined the first one. "Stupid!" Suddenly I had a whole audience of first-graders calling Cat-a-lion stupid. This was not the response I anticipated.

This incident was a powerful lesson for me about how children often imitate behavior they observe in real life, in play, and even—for better or worse—in the media. When I play with children, I am always careful about how my puppets behave. For instance, they are vocal about their displeasure about getting shots or undergoing whatever medical procedures the children imagine for them—but they always cooperate with the doctors and nurses. They refrain from hitting, biting, or calling people names. At the same time, my puppets own and identify their feelings and are articulate about what they like and what they don't like.

For me, being able to engage children in pretend play has been invaluable as a means of helping them deal with often extreme situations. But it's important to remember that such play has benefits for children coping with the slings and arrows of everyday living as well. Life can have difficult moments even for kids who aren't facing extraordinary illnesses, hospitalizations, or family upheavals. The changes occurring in the normal course of growing up—including transitions from crib to bed, from diapers to a potty, from only child to sibling, from preschool to kindergarten—can be very stressful.

Take Michael, for example, a five-year-old who learned he would soon be graduating from a preschool where he'd been happily ensconced for over half of his life.

I began working with Michael because a few of the children in his class were having rather severe problems and I occasionally brought my puppets to perform for the whole class. Although he was actually in fine shape emotionally and physically, Michael's fascination with my puppets spurred his teachers and me to add him to the roster of children with whom I worked individually each week. It was a restful and delightful experience—and it turned out that I was able to help Michael during a difficult time for him. In doing so I learned a lot about the ways play can help children coping with ordinary rather than extraordinary challenges.

At five, Michael had a sunny disposition. He acted out wonderfully elaborate fantasies in our sessions. One day, however, his play seemed mechanized and joyless. He smashed a dinosaur and engaged in other fantasy violence. He laughed and said that I should tell the puppets that he was just joking. But his laughter seemed forced and he certainly didn't look happy.

I knew that something was bothering him, but I couldn't figure out what and he wasn't very communicative. Finally I had to tell him that our time together was ending and that I would see him next week. "I know that!" said Michael quickly. "*I* didn't know that!" Audrey responded. "Phooey!!"

Michael told me to make Audrey angry because he was leaving, and that's when we finally got to the heart of what was bothering him.

MICHAEL: Audrey's supposed to get mad because I have to leave.

AUDREY: I'm mad because Michael has to go!

MICHAEL (*suddenly and with great feeling*): I wish this was my school so I could stay here forever and ever.

AUDREY (*equally heartfelt*): I wish this was my school so I could stay here forever and ever. I wish I didn't have to graduate or anything!

MICHAEL: I wish I didn't have to go to kindergarten. I wish I can never ever ever leave this place. I don't want to leave this place. This is my best school. I love this school!

AUDREY: I like day care! I don't want to move.

MICHAEL: Why should everything have to stop? We're playing some game and we have to stop. Why do I have to play some game and then we have to stop?

AUDREY: I don't like it when things stop!

MICHAEL: Yeah! Every time I want to do this, I can't even see you. All I can do is dream about you. Every time I dream of something I feel like you're not there. And now we have to stop.

AUDREY (*sadly*): A lot of things are stopping.

MICHAEL: I hate that.

AUDREY: Me too.

Once Michael got started, his feelings came rushing out in a flood. It turned out that he wasn't just sad about leaving day care—he had specific fears about what was in store for him at his new school. "Why do I have to go to kindergarten when I'm just like this [I think he meant that he was small] and kids are going to push me around?" he asked. Audrey replied, "That sounds scary!"

This was the first time Michael talked about his impending

separation from day care. Because working through difficult issues isn't usually an instantaneous experience, it was a theme that he introduced repeatedly in the coming weeks.

"Wait!" he exclaimed one day. "I have a good idea! If I have a girlfriend at school, maybe she'll kiss me and that will make me much better!" Audrey was puzzled. "If she kisses you, it will make you better?" "Yeah," Michael enthused. "Yeah, if she kisses me, she'll tell me I'm cute. Yeah! That's a great idea! Man, I'm gonna love kindergarten!" He heaved a sigh of relief.

I didn't know where Michael's notion that having a girlfriend would make him powerful came from, but he came from a culture in which men and women were expected to behave in rather rigidly prescribed roles. Like many young children today, he was casually exposed to a great deal of media meant for teenagers and adults and this may well have fed his fantasies. In fact, having a girlfriend and exploring gender roles occupied a great deal of Michael's playtime, but I decided, to begin with, to focus on and reinforce the core truth behind his fantasy: "If someone cares about you, places don't seem so scary," Audrey mused.

From an adult's perspective, Michael's graduation from day care may be seen as merely part of the normal flow of life. We know that he would get bored returning year after year and that children need new challenges as they grow and develop. But from Michael's perspective, he was being yanked—without his consent—out of a comfortable, safe environment where everyone knew him and loved him, only to be plopped into a situation that he perceived as dangerous. Why wouldn't he be anxious and angry?

At the beginning of our next session, Michael attacked the cushions with increased vigor, employing stylized karate kicks and appropriate sound effects. He explained between kicks that they were "bad guys." My goal was to help him find a more constructive outlet for his anger and for expressing his fears about leaving. I decided to have Audrey verbalize the feelings that he was expressing nonverbally as though they were her own.

"Boy," said Audrey, "when I'm angry, I feel like doing that. But I don't want to hurt anybody." Michael intensified his kicking. "The bad guys can cook you!" he huffed. "They cook you up for dinner!" Audrey repeated what she had said earlier: "Sometimes when I'm mad I feel like doing that too. But I don't. I say, 'I'm mad!' instead."

Michael stopped kicking. "Say that again," he commanded. Audrey yelled, "I'm mad!" "You *are* mad!" Michael commented. "You look mad." "Guess why I'm mad," said Audrey. "Because I'm fighting," answered Michael, and he resumed his kickboxing. But Audrey disagreed. "I'm mad because I'm going to be leaving here at the end of the summer," she announced with feeling. Michael suddenly stopped kicking and looked at Audrey. "Are you sure?" he asked. He turned to me, "Is Audrey sure?" Audrey nodded her head.

Often when Audrey is in a conflict with another puppet, children will urge her to hit, or bite, or kick. Because imitation of any actions they see others perform is such a strong component of how children learn and because having them physicalize their anger by hurting someone else would signal approval of that behavior, my puppets are never violent. They do, however, acknowledge their very strong feelings. Sometimes they even acknowledge that they *feel* like hitting, or kicking, or biting, but choose to exercise self-control instead.

While kicking cushions was certainly better than kicking another person, it wasn't adding to Michael's repertoire of coping skills, so I decided to continue to have Audrey verbalize "her" feelings about leaving preschool. In doing so, I was hoping to give Michael permission to talk about what was bothering him and to help him find the language to do so.

Engaging in make believe with children—speaking through fantasy creatures or assuming a fantasy role—gives us a chance to introduce important points of view that they might not be able, or willing, to hear directly, and to expose them to alternative ways of coping. By attributing feelings of anger to Audrey, I could address what I was pretty sure was bothering Michael without putting him on the spot or forcing him to own up to feelings he wasn't ready to acknowledge.

More than once I've been asked if I am, in essence, "putting feelings into children's heads" when my puppets express strong negative emotions. But my experience suggests this is not the case. If I'm off base, the children let me know by ignoring the feelings Audrey has expressed, or even by explicitly distancing themselves from them by saying something like, "*I* don't feel sad." Nor am I suggesting that we should push children to acknowledge feelings before they are ready to do so. Still, the experience of hearing feelings acknowledged and accepted is important, and the fact that it's a puppet—and not them—expressing those feelings makes it safe.

Suppose I wasn't really sure about how Michael was feeling about leaving preschool? When that happens, I'll say something like, "Audrey, how do you feel about going to a new school?" And Audrey will reply, "I don't even know how I'm feeling." I'll turn to the child and say, "How do you think Audrey's feeling?" Usually—but not always—children respond by telling me how *they* are feeling.

Because the thought of children being frightened or unhappy is hard to bear for the adults who care for them, we often minimize the depth of their responses to life events. But haven't we all experienced various degrees of anger, grief, and fear in response to transitions, losses, separations, and injustices? Actually, when they feel safe to do so, children usually communicate their feelings quite clearly, one way or another. Given his sullen demeanor and the vigor with which he was attacking those pillows, it was not a big leap to assume that Michael was angry. My goal for Michael was to let him know that it was understandable that he was having those feelings, and to help him find ways of expressing them without hurting himself or other people.

"I'm going to graduate at the end of the summer," said Michael sadly, and he resumed kicking the cushions.

Once again Audrey expressed her anger about leaving. Michael came over and gave her a hug. "I'm never going to see you again," he sighed. "That makes me so-o-o sad," said Audrey. "You're going to a new place." Michael nodded solemnly. "And I don't want to do it," he said. "It makes me mad."

After he and Audrey commiserated about their upcoming departures, Michael had more to say about where he was going. "Why do we have to go to a new place?" he griped. "All the little people are going to hit me. They're going to punch my face." Audrey commiserated. "That's what I'm scared about— that people are going to punch me." "They're gonna call me a fat boy!" Michael added. "Yeah," Audrey agreed. "They'll call you a fat boy and me a fat girl. I'm scared about that." Michael nodded again and said, "I'm scared about that. I don't want a bully to come tell me I'm stinky." "Yeah," said Audrey. "I don't want a bully to do that to me either."

I wasn't sure where Michael was getting his ideas about life in kindergarten, so I asked him a question: "What makes you think that's going to happen to you after you graduate?" Michael replied promptly: "Every time I go back to a new school, people will punch me in the face, call me a fat boy, fight with me. Every dude! Every thing! Make me have blood in my mouth."

I also didn't know whether something like this had really happened to Michael, or if this was simply what he was afraid was going to happen. When I asked him directly if he had ever been teased or hurt by other kids he shook his head. We started to talk about what to do if he actually encountered a bully. At this point, Michael had a question for Audrey.

"What would happen if a big monster came up to you and told you that 'I'm going to cook you up'?" he asked. "What would you do then?" When Audrey answered that she would find a grown-up to help her, Michael became skeptical and rather threatening. "Oh, yeah? I gotta man who was here . . . you would sure be upset. He can beat anything up. He can, he can beat anyone up and beat and beat and beat them up." Audrey was impressed. "Is he a grown-up or a kid?" "A kid," Michael explained cheerfully. "He's four. His name is B.J. He can beat anyone up! He's the bestest beater in the world!"

I tried to bring Michael back to the question of what he would do if he encountered a bully at kindergarten and suggested that he use his new teachers as resources if he was frightened, but he wouldn't even hear of it. He had other things on his mind.

MICHAEL: Why should I go to some stupid—to some stupid school?

ME: To some stupid school?

MICHAEL: Yeah, why should I go to some stupid school?

AUDREY: Yeah, why should I do that? Why should I go to some stupid school?

MICHAEL: Yeah, how come I go to some stupid place, stupid place, and have to—and have to stay there forever and ever and ever?

AUDREY: Will Michael still be living with his mom when he goes to a different school?

ME: Sure. Of course.

MICHAEL (*with confidence*): I'm *always* going to be living with my mom. Audrey, will you be living with your mom?

AUDREY: Uh-huh.

ME: So that'll be the same, but you won't be *here*.

AUDREY: But why?

ME: 'Cause you guys are growing up and you're getting older and the day care doesn't have a kindergarten program.

MICHAEL: And when you turn six, you can stop growing.

ME: Mnunhmmm. You're growing all the time.

MICHAEL: You grow like my dad. My dad is sooooo big!

AUDREY: You're so strong, huh?

MICHAEL: And now I'm going to show you something really, really, really cool.

He lifted a cylindrical cushion over his head as if it were a heavy weight, then pranced around impersonating a strongman while Audrey oohed and aahed. I think it was no accident that Michael, who was feeling particularly small and vulnerable at the thought of his new school, transformed himself into a strongman. When faced with challenging situations, children often use pretend play to experience being stronger and braver and more powerful than they are in real life.

By the time children—boys in particular—are four or five, they have picked up the prevailing societal message that admitting to being afraid, or feeling weak or frightened, is not acceptable. Like many adults, a child grappling with a challenging or scary situation may need to save face. Had I said, "Michael, I know you're feeling weak and powerless right now," there is a strong likelihood that he would have denied it. He might even have gotten hurt or angry. Instead, because we were "just" playing together, I could assign those same feelings to Audrey Duck.

> AUDREY: You know what? I feel like if I could just get stronger, I'd be safer at kindergarten.
> ME: Audrey, you know, I want to tell you something. Everybody kind of gets scared when they go to a new school for the first time.
> AUDREY: *Everybody* gets scared when they go to a new school?
> ME: Everybody.

Michael visibly relaxed as he listened to our conversation. By talking with Audrey about "her" feelings and reassuring Audrey that lots of kids felt the same way about going to a new school, I was able to reassure Michael too. In addition, by using Audrey to say what I knew Michael was feeling but couldn't or wouldn't express, I was able to let him see that I was willing to talk about difficult feelings, and that I wasn't angry at Audrey for having them.

Michael began playing with Audrey's hair. He piled it on top of her head. "How do I look?" she asked. "Good!" he answered, giving her a big hug. "Now you're the blues."

Audrey was puzzled. "I'm the blues?" she asked. "You have to sing a song into the blues," Michael explained. "Oh," said Audrey. "I understand. How does it go?"

After a dramatic pause, Michael held a pretend microphone to his lips and began to sing: "Ohhhhhh, I got the blues!" Then he stopped. Holding the mic in front of Audrey, he announced that *she* had to sing. And so she did:

> I got the blues.
> 'Cause I'm leaving day care and I don't want to.
> I want to stay here,
> For-ever
> And not go to kindergarten.
> I got the blues. I got the leaving-day-care blues.

"Now it's my turn," Michael announced. He picked up the tempo and began to sing with gusto:

> I got the blues, blues, blues,
> and every time, I do this . . . every day,
> I got the blues.

The more he sang, the more he became like a real blues singer. Half chanting, half singing, always in perfect tempo, he threw himself into his song.

> Every time! I do the blues.
> (*Spoken.*) The blues clues, man.
> Every time! I got the blues.
> I don't want to leave school.
> Every time I leave to school,
> Every time, I do the bluuuues.

After a few more lines, Michael turned to Audrey. "Now, it's your turn to be the blues," he ordered. Obediently, Audrey began singing, and he joined her in a duet, playing Louis Armstrong to her Ella Fitzgerald.

AUDREY: I've got the blues. I got the blues.
I've got the missing-Michael blues.
MICHAEL: Ba-by. I got the Michael-missing blues.
AUDREY: I got the blues.
I'm missing Michael,
'Cause I know he's got to gra-du-ate.
MICHAEL: 'Cause he's gra-du-atin' . . .
AUDREY: Yeah! And, going on to kin-der-gar-ten,
And I'll miss him
But I'm glad he's gonna go,
'Cause it means he's growing up.
And that's a good thing.
MICHAEL: 'Cause I know he's growin' up
To be a better kid.
AUDREY: I'm going to miss him. I'm so sad.
And I know that I like Michael,
And I am gonna miss him.
MICHAEL: And I gotta know he's a big boy.

Michael, clearly pleased with himself, decided that he now needed an official introduction. He informed Audrey that she needed to introduce him. "You have to hold the microphone," he directed. "Then you're s'posed to say, 'Ladies and gentlemen, let's put your hands together for Michael.' No! Wait!" He interrupted himself. "Wait a minute," he said. "Audrey, before you say that, you have to say, 'It's the amazing—the blues guy—Dr. Michael!'"

Audrey did the best she could. Her voice became soft and mellow: "Ladies and gentlemen. We are in for a special treat tonight. Put your hands together for the greatest blues guy, Dr. Michael. Yeaaaa! Here he comes! Yeaaaaa!"

Michael ran out, looking momentarily more like Shaquille O'Neal on the basketball court than a blues singer taking the stage. But he got back into it. Writhing with emotion, twisting his torso around the microphone, he attacked the blues even more ferociously than before:

Every TIME, I talk about the blues
Every DAY, I talk about the blues
Every time, I know that Audrey is going away.
But that's okay, 'cause she's my best friend,
And I'm gonna miss her every time.

His voice dropped to a dramatic whisper. He pointed his finger, stretching his arm out to an imaginary audience, and swiveled around. He was every inch a bluesman: "Stick a-round!"

But then suddenly he was a five-year-old boy again. "I need to use the bathroom," he said, and raced out of the room.

Until we actually said good-bye, Michael continued to play out his leave-taking, but he no longer seemed to feel the need to punch and kick and he did well in his new school. As adults, it's often hard for us to remember the emotional experience of being a child, and in any case, the children we love are not little replicas of us—they may well respond to life's challenges with concerns and feelings that are different from our own. At the same time, they look to us for guidance about how to cope and—for better or worse—they often model their behavior after ours. Because children naturally use make believe to make sense of and work through whatever they happen to be grappling with, observing their play can give us a sense of what's on their minds—even concerns that they may be unable or unwilling to talk about directly. While Audrey Duck shared and validated Michael's anger and fear about leaving day care, *I* made sure that she used words—not violence—to express those feelings.

I find that, when given the opportunity, children seem to grasp intuitively that make believe can be a safe space for self-expression and for working through life's challenges. It's up to us to provide children with the kind of physical and psychological space where pretend play thrives—what I think of as Winnicott's "holding environment."

But long before I worked with Michael, I learned an ironic lesson about creating a holding environment for children to play in: clearly defined boundaries and limits are essential to the freedoms afforded by make believe.

6

Joey, Olivia, and Emma

Limits, Boundaries, and the Freedom to Play

As I walk into the Corner Co-op Nursery School one day I see one of the teachers, Beth, scrunched up in a corner. "You're in jail," shouts five-year-old Brian, building a wall of blocks at her feet. "Forever!" Beth obligingly pleads to be let out of jail, but Brian is adamant. "You're in jail!" he repeats excitedly and raises his hand to hit her. Beth, instantly transforming herself from cowering prisoner to calm adult, tells him that he can't hit. Brian—momentarily a little boy again—nods his head and effortlessly resumes his role as jailor as Beth returns to cowering. Brian grabs a peaked jester's hat with bells sewn onto it and twirls it with reckless abandon over his head, narrowly missing a little girl who happens to be passing by. Once again Beth transforms from prisoner to teacher. "We can't swing the hat like that," she says calmly to Brian, "because the bells on the end could hurt someone." Brian stops swinging the hat and returns to his block wall, launching into a litany of the terrible things that will happen to Beth while she's a prisoner. "You're going to be there forever!" he says. He's thinking hard. "And it's always going to be dark!" he adds. "And," his voice gets louder, "you're going to have *nothing* to cuddle with!" Beth returns to cowering and their play together continues.

Children can play only when they feel safe. When they feel unsafe, they stop playing. It's the role of the adults who care for them to ensure their physical and emotional safety. One of the ways we do this, as I learned from a seven-year-old named Joey, is to help them clarify the boundaries between reality and fantasy and to respect those boundaries once they are set.

Joey's sister died at 5:47 on a bleak Tuesday morning in March, less than three days after the doctors transplanted some of Joey's bone marrow into her body in an unsuccessful attempt to save her life. By 4:35 that afternoon, Joey and the rest of his family would be flying back down south, hundreds of miles away, to bury Laura and begin their lives without her. I would never see him again.

I had known Joey for almost three weeks and I thought that it was important for him that we meet once more, if only to say good-bye. At the very least, I wanted him to know that I would miss him and that I was sad about Laura's death. Joey and his mother and his twelve-year-old brother were staying in a rooming house across the street from the hospital. I didn't know his mother well, and the thought of telephoning her, of intruding on her grief to arrange details about where and when I would see Joey, was distasteful to me. Still, I made the call.

We arranged that Joey's aunt would bring him over to the hospital after breakfast. As I hung up the phone, I felt a wave of uncertainty. What could I *say* to a seven-year-old whose sister died of leukemia after he gave up a part of himself to try to save her? Would he meet with me again only because his mother wanted him to, or would this last piece of work together have meaning for him? Our regular meeting place had been a little office down the hall from the room where Laura had been treated. Would that be a good choice because of its familiarity? Or would returning to the floor be frightening for him? Would the medical staff want him back there, or would he be a painful reminder of their failure to save a life? Should I bring my puppets? Would he be able to use them? If not, what could I say to him directly that would help?

Jean, the head nurse on the unit, assured me that Joey was welcome to come back. He and I took the elevator up to the fifth floor and walked to Jean's tiny, glass-walled office, made private by posters of kittens and baby chicks, as well as countless snapshots of happy-looking children, some of whom were still actually living.

Previously, when Joey wasn't using puppets his manner had been markedly offhand and controlled. But the intensity and ferociousness of his puppet play revealed the depth of the terror, helplessness, and rage he felt about his sister's illness and his role in her treatment: he enacted mutilations, horrible illnesses, medical procedures, and attacks by dragons, juxtaposed with baby sharks, baby talk, and puppets being teased for "acting like a baby." Today Joey was pale and composed, but the rigidity of his shoulders eloquently communicated his tension. "I wish there were someone here with me," I thought, "to help me help this child."

As soon as we closed the door behind us, I told Joey that I felt sad about Laura. He began to fidget and ask questions about the office. He wondered why the two posters were there. He wondered whose coat was thrown over a chair. He wondered aloud about all sorts of safe and meaningless things. I was used to Joey asking these kinds of questions when there was something too painful to talk about.

I noticed that he had a new chain around his neck and I asked him about it. He pulled out a heart-shaped locket made out of gold-colored metal. "It was for Laura," he said. "I was going to give it to her." He shrugged his shoulders and opened his eyes wide. "Now I'll have to find someone else to give it to." He sounded so casual about it, but I was reminded of the first time I'd met him.

"Joey," I had said, as usual, "my name is Susan and I have some puppets. I talk to kids in the hospital who are sick, or sometimes to the brothers and sisters of kids who are sick. This is a time when you can talk about, or play about, your feelings about being here, or anything else." "Oh," Joey had replied, "I don't have any more feelings. I've already talked to two people about them and I don't have any more."

During the next three weeks, however, he proceeded to reveal his anguish, fears, and fantasies through his play. Puppets were devoured, operated on, died, and returned as ghosts. Hungry dragons threatened Audrey Duck and Cat-a-lion daily. He made Audrey swallow a piranha, then made Cat-a-lion die trying to save her by swallowing the piranha himself. All of this from a child who said he didn't have any more feelings.

Now Joey and I were quiet for a while and I saw him staring at the bag of puppets I'd brought. At the bottom, showing through the clear plastic, was the puppet he had always chosen to use—a fuzzy yellow frog. I could see Joey looking at the frog and waited for him to speak.

"What's that yellow thing?" he asked. I understood then that we would indeed be playing with puppets.

I shouldn't have been surprised. Joey wanted to communicate in the same way we had been communicating so intensely since we'd met. Perversely, and despite all my experience working with children in this way, it made me uncomfortable.

"Laura is dead," I thought. "For real. And now we're going to *play* about it?" For a long moment I thought that the tragedy and irreversibility of his sister's death made playing seem so pointless and trivial. The fact that puppets are not "really" alive, and therefore cannot die for real, made using them in the context of an actual death that had just taken place seem like a hollow and meaningless gesture.

I was wrong. I was being unfair to Joey, who had a right to decide how we spent our time together and who needed to cope with Laura's death in his own way. I was there to help him do that, not to tell him how. Laura's death was a part of Joey's life. His feelings about her death, her illness, and his participation in her treatment were powerful and alive. They needed to be somehow expressed and assimilated for him to continue to grow and develop. It is a rare seven-year-old for whom language alone is adequate for this task. Joey *needed* to play.

Joey put on the fuzzy yellow puppet, whom he had long since identified as a baby frog, and said, "Hi." I put on Cat-a-lion and had him say "Hi" back.

Joey turned to me accusingly. "Why is his voice different?" he demanded. "It sounds sort of soft and low." I commented that I thought his own voice sounded a little like that. "No, it doesn't," Joey retorted loudly.

I tried making Cat-a-lion answer back, "My voice is low because I feel sad about Laura." But Joey would have none of that. "How does *he* know?" he asked skeptically. Finally I put Cat-a-lion down for a minute, looked directly at Joey, and said, "I think his voice is so low because I'm making him talk. I feel sad about Laura, so *my* voice sounds low. I think we all feel sad about Laura."

Then I said that I wanted to talk to him about something that didn't have anything to do with puppets. I said that sometimes kids think it's their fault when they give bone marrow to someone and that person dies, but Laura was very, very sick before that and her death didn't have anything to do with his bone marrow. Joey nodded. Then he began to play in earnest.

He made the dragon puppet attack Cat-a-lion. He roared after both Cat-a-lion and Audrey Duck. He terrorized them. He said that Cat-a-lion couldn't walk. He said they both needed blood tests and proceeded to administer them.

After a series of more blood tests, Joey started shaving the puppets' heads, just as Laura's head had been shaved. Then he gave them more and more injections with a vigor that became increasingly ferocious.

I had recently stopped letting children perform medical procedures on my puppets unless they could state a reason for them. In theory this makes sense. It is certainly important for adult caretakers to do everything they can to help children understand that there *is* a reason for the discomfort they suffer in the hospital. What differentiates a hospital from a house of torture is the positive purpose behind the pain administered and the motives of the people working there who genuinely care about their patients. One way to reinforce this point with children is to model this caring in puppet play when the occasion arises.

However, when I asked Joey why Cat-a-lion was getting so many shots he cried wildly, "For no reason! A shot for no reason! A bundle of shots for no reason! A hundred shots for no reason!" I didn't push him. Releasing his feelings, expressing his fear and rage, was more important than anything else right then. Besides, he had in fact undergone what must have seemed like hundreds of shots and blood tests for what seemed like no reason—Laura was dead anyway.

Joey pretended to cut Cat-a-lion up. With great gusto, he pretended to cut off Cat-a-lion's tongue, his whiskers, his eyes, and anything else he could think of removing. He was very in-tent on this mutilation and appeared to enjoy it immensely.

I chose to encourage this enjoyment. I matched my tone to his demeanor and kept my voice playfully casual. "Oh, no! Cat-a-lion sure is having a bad time today." I shook my head and joined Joey in his laughter. I wanted him to know that I recognized the intensity of his play but that this outpouring of rage wasn't really hurting anyone. Especially because I was never going to see Joey again, I wanted to let him simply express what he needed to express without probing for connections between his play and the depth of his feelings.

I could have used Cat-a-lion to verbalize the feelings of fear and helplessness experienced by so many children in hospitals. I could have spoken directly or through a puppet about the anger Joey was acting out. If I had known I was going to be working with Joey over a long period of time, I might have used these and other methods to encourage him to reflect on what he was doing. But in making an on-the-spot decision about how to respond at this moment I needed to take into consideration not only my understanding of what this play meant to Joey but also the context of the play: I was never going to see Joey again and I didn't want our last encounter to add to his pain by opening up wounds that I wouldn't be around to help him close.

Also contributing to my decision to reinforce the playfulness of Joey's fantasy was the obvious precariousness of his capacity to play at all at this most difficult time. After each expression of violent mutilation he talked about stopping—said he wanted to stop—but kept on playing even when I supported his decision to quit.

In a last flight of fancy, Joey invented a machine that

chopped up fruit, meat, and teeth. When I commented that I had never heard of a machine that cut up teeth, he suddenly said, "And anyway, I don't know why Laura's still here, in that room."

"I don't know that she is," I answered. "But maybe they're getting ready to take her back down south."

"They're going to bury her next to my other sister," Joey said. "The doctors didn't take good care of her. She died when she had an operation or something."

"I think that the doctors and nurses here did take good care of Laura," I answered.

"Well, they tried to," said Joey.

I let Joey know that we had about five more minutes together. He examined his arm, which was covered with pink and purple paint as well as puncture marks and bruises. I commented that the shots and procedures he had endured had caused the black-and-blue marks, but not the purple or pink paint splatters.

"The pink is pee-pee," Joey commented, offering me a guilty look. I laughed but did not voice the connection between pink pee-pee and how he had told me a few days ago that he heard the doctors talking about finding blood in Laura's urine. Our time together was ending and pointing out that connection would have been an opening for more discussion. Instead we needed closure. We put the puppets away and took the elevator downstairs to the lobby.

We said good-bye at the hospital gift shop, where Joey's mother was waiting for him. I left them standing in line to buy a coloring book for the long plane ride home. Joey stood there patiently, a shaggy-haired, stocky little boy with a pale, dirt-streaked face, wearing a purple T-shirt several sizes too big and a gold-colored locket around his neck.

To enable freedom of expression in play we must define its limits. The limits of play become a container within which we are safely and therefore uninhibitedly able to create. These boundaries—a definition of the safe environment in which play takes place—are crucial for providing the sense of security necessary for honest self-expression.

We build a fence around a playground in order to keep children from wandering off. We childproof a playroom to keep them from physical harm. A psychological play space also needs limits and boundaries to keep children safe from confusion, overstimulation, and emotional harm. When children play alone they set these boundaries naturally. When we play with them, we create these boundaries by making clear distinctions between reality and fantasy, and by setting consistent limits.

When I talk about "reality" for the purposes of understanding make believe, I am talking about the reality and validity of feelings in our inner lives as well as about all of that which belongs to the world outside of ourselves. In this sense, play is simultaneously, and precariously, real and not real. The themes and feelings expressed are real, but the contents—the characters and what happens to them—are fantasy.

When a child plays alone, the delineation of these boundaries is totally within his or her control. When I engage a child in puppet play to encourage self-expression, to provide an opportunity to overcome feelings of helplessness, or to teach positive coping skills, I must be attuned to the child's boundaries and respect them, otherwise our interaction ceases to be play.

In Joey's case, by making an explicit connection between the difference he astutely perceived in Cat-a-lion's voice (the fantasy play) and that which I heard in his own voice (reality),

I transgressed the boundaries Joey had established and momentarily threatened his capacity to play. I knew as soon as Joey so uncharacteristically balked at entering into play with Cat-a-lion that using a puppet to talk directly about Laura's death was a misstep on my part. Laura really did die. Her death was not play. Therefore, any discussion of her death needed to come from me, as myself, and not from the puppets. If, however, Joey had introduced Laura's death into the play—if *he* began to talk about it directly through puppets—I would have followed his lead.

When a child is playing less directly about something that seems particularly frightening or intense, such as the death of a parent, I might remind him or her that we are playing. "Your mother's dead," says a five-year-old girl to Audrey, her eyes growing bigger and bigger. "Your mother's *dead*." "We're pretending that Audrey Duck's mother is dead," I respond in my own voice, just to make sure that the boundaries are intact and to remind her that this is play and therefore under her control.

Confident in the reversibility of their actions within the safety of our shared fantasy, children have pretended to do horrendous things to my puppets. They have been devoured by monsters, burned at the stake, and left to drown while a parent watches passively from the shore. Children are able to commit these atrocities because they know that what we do with the puppets is pretend—after our play session the characters will be removed from our hands only to return intact during another play session.

Another way of ensuring that the boundaries of fantasy play remain clear is to be selective about whom we engage in this process. For many children, if the content they create starts to become overwhelming, gentle but vigilant reminders that they are playing is enough to preserve the safety of their play. For others, however, because of the depth of an emotional trauma or the presence of psychosis, pretend play is so evocative that the line between reality and fantasy seems too tenuous for make believe to be helpful to them.

Age is also a factor. Children mature at different rates, but in my experience most three-year-olds—particularly three-year-olds under stress—tend to be dubious candidates for puppet therapy. Children this young can sometimes be scared of puppets that are animated from within. We use handheld standing dolls and tell stories *about* them, letting the child see us moving them—not in the puppet's own voice—for the younger child. When children are under severe stress, they can temporarily lose some of the cognitive, social, and emotional gains they've made, and they often act and react like much younger children.

Assiduously sorting out the differences between reality and fantasy seems to be a primary developmental task for most of the three-year-olds I've encountered. Children younger than three seem to firmly believe that my puppets are "real"; children older than three seem to be pretty secure in the knowledge that they are not. But three-year-olds tend to be skeptical—and the fact that they aren't sure about whether the puppets are really talking bothers them. Almost every three-year-old I have worked with in a hospital setting has devoted most of our time together to arguing with me about the puppets. They ask me how the puppets talk and then they don't believe the answer. I say that I'm making Audrey talk. They strongly disagree. I show them. They still don't believe me. And so on.

Yet I have often been asked to work with three-year-olds. From the point of view of hospital staff, this makes sense. The younger the child, the more difficult it is to explain the value and purpose of painful, invasive procedures and the more the staff needs help. "She's really cute!" a nurse would say enticingly, or, "He's really smart—and so verbal!" This last is from a cardiology resident. (Cuteness, of course, is irrelevant in assessing a child's capacity to benefit from puppet play, but it's harder to see that, for very young children, being "so verbal" is usually irrelevant too.)

A verbally skilled three-year-old is still only—gloriously and tenaciously—a three-year-old, as I discovered for the umpteenth time with Olivia, an extremely precocious little girl hospitalized for a kidney disease that was serious but curable.

When I first met Olivia, she separated from her mother easily and we began to play in the usual way. I introduced her to Audrey Duck and handed her some puppets for her own use. Olivia stared at Audrey for a long moment and said, "How does she talk?" "I make her talk," I said and continued to do so. After a few minutes, Olivia did speak directly to Audrey, but not to begin playing. "How do you talk?" she asked, continuing to stare intently. "Susan makes me talk," replied Audrey Duck.

By the time Olivia repeated her question for a third time, I realized that the answer just wasn't sinking in. "I make Audrey talk," I said again. "Like this," and I showed her how I did it. "Just like you can make your puppets talk." I helped her put on an elephant. She transferred her intent gaze to the puppet on her right hand. "Talk!" she commanded. Then she smiled at me and whispered confidentially, "Mine don't talk."

We spent the next few minutes repeating variations on this process. Finally Olivia began to whimper for her mother. Unfortunately, unbeknown to us, her mother had taken this opportunity to slip away to the hospital coffee shop. Upon hearing this, I had what I thought was a brilliant idea. "Let's pretend that Audrey Duck's mother went down for coffee!" I suggested. It seemed like a natural. Olivia would be able to express her feelings about her mother's absence and maybe act out a series of departures and reunions. A huge smile broke through Olivia's sadness. "Okay," she agreed, and held up the elephant expectantly.

"My mother went down for coffee," announced Audrey Duck. "And I'm mad and I'm sad, but I know she's coming back." A long silence followed. Olivia put down the elephant, looked long and hard at me, and then turned to Audrey. "You're only a puppet," she announced. "You don't even *have* a mother!"

What's wrong with this picture? Here was an articulate, friendly, interested three-year-old who was perfectly willing to interact but could not sustain make believe with me. In spite of my persistent efforts to clarify the reality-fantasy boundary for her, she was not ready to have it clarified. She was ready to think about it—in fact, sorting out this issue seemed to be of primary importance to her—but she was not yet sure enough to put the question aside, so the puppets were useless to her as tools of expression or coping.

Pretend play can place stress on behavioral boundaries as well as on those associated with reality and fantasy. Puppets in particular are valuable for self-expression because they loosen inhibitions. But just as children can be overwhelmed by frightening fantasies if they lose sight of the fact that they are not real, they can also be overwhelmed if pretend play—tapping feelings of rage or fear—leads them to physical violence. For safe self-expression, the boundaries of any kind of make believe need to include limits on behavior. As I've mentioned earlier, the limits I set with children are simple: "It's okay to be angry, but you can't use the puppets to hit."

This is a straightforward rule, but its successful implementation involves some thought. When a child and an adult are playing with puppets, an adult's response is frequently to try to set and enforce rules through the puppets themselves. This evolves into a rapidly deteriorating scenario that sounds like this:

> CHILD'S PUPPET: I'm going to get you! (*Begins attacking adult's puppet.*)
> ADULT'S PUPPET: Don't hit me! Don't hit me!
> CHILD'S PUPPET (*continues slugging with increased vigor and excitement*): I'm going to get you! I'm going to get you!

Equally unsuccessful is any attempt to elicit a child's sympathy for the puppet at that particular moment. A comment such as "Audrey Duck doesn't like to be hit" usually elicits a blank stare, a shrug, and continued violence.

The problem with both of these responses is that they are confusing to children because puppets are playthings. Everything that comes out of a puppet's mouth is make believe. When a puppet yells, "It hurts! It hurts!" children assume (rightly) that we are pretending that the puppet is hurting and therefore there is no reason to stop the attack. The admonishment "Audrey doesn't like to be hit" is equally fantastical.

Now, when a child begins to hit my puppets, I've learned to respond, "It's okay to be angry, but you can't hit." When pressed for a reason, I tell the truth: "Because my hand is in there, and *I* don't like to be hit." For most children, the truth is enough. For some children, those who have trouble controlling aggressive impulses, for instance, the uninhibiting nature of puppets—the very thing that makes them such a powerful therapeutic tool—is too evocative and threatening. Puppet play ceases to be play and rapidly becomes something uncontrollable and dangerously overwhelming. In these instances, I put the puppets away and try an activity more structured and less provocative.

Once a safe play space has been established, however, the child's creation is sacrosanct. I contribute to the play, I may try to structure it around a particular theme, but the children are free to respond to my contributions in any way they choose, and to initiate their own themes and content. As much as possible, the child leads and I follow.

I have followed children through horrendous make believe terrain, rife with hungry dragons, angry dinosaurs, cruel witches, and crueler doctors. Especially for children under stress, the way is often fraught with fantasies of rage and destruction, and the content of our play is sometimes difficult for parents who have an investment in seeing their children as good through and through. I understand this. I can, and do, bear the unhappiness, anger, fear, or misbehavior of lots of children, but it's always much harder with those to whom I am related, so I sympathize with other parents who cringe at their children's angry fantasies.

On one memorable occasion I worked with four-year-old Emma, who was hospitalized for an intestinal disorder. She was sweet and charming and the delight of her father, who was rather disconcerted to witness what he perceived to be her abuse of Audrey Duck.

Emma carefully wiped off Audrey's wing and explained to her that she needed to have a shot. She then pretended to give Audrey a long and obviously extremely painful injection, during which I made Audrey cry. When the torturous procedure was finally done, Emma took Audrey in her arms and soothed her cries. "There, there," she murmured, stroking Audrey's back.

As her father watched with growing horror, Emma repeated this scenario over and over and over again. Finally he couldn't stand it any more. "Emma!" he cried. "Isn't that enough?" "No," said Emma calmly and proceeded to administer yet another long and painful injection.

Afterward, I took Emma's father aside to explain the difference between fantasy play that contains violent images or approximates violent actions and play that deteriorates into actual violence. From my point of view, which includes recognition of the powerful feelings of rage that children often experience during hospitalization or other life crises, Emma's play was a healthy, intense, and wholly acceptable outlet for feelings she was not getting an opportunity to express otherwise. By safely channeling those feelings into play that had clear boundaries, she could actively express her anger without hurting herself or anyone else, and she could simultaneously communicate about and gain some mastery over her experience. It was a way for her to process and get some control over a complex and uncomfortable situation. To understand and feel comfortable with the content of Emma's fantasy play, however, her father had to acknowledge and respect the intensity of her emotions and the reality of her rage. That's a hard thing to do with the children we love, whether they are facing extraordinary stress or the normal challenges of life.

It's a paradox that setting limits and boundaries is essential for children to feel safe enough to freely engage in pretend play. Another paradox is that make believe is a way—occasionally the only way—for children to truly be themselves. Even as they pretend to be someone else, or to be themselves in fantasy circumstances, children are expressing real thoughts, real concerns, and real feelings.

7

Kara

The Truth in Make Believe

As a child, I turned to puppets instinctively to preserve myself from a somewhat overbearing family and from a world that, at the height of the cold war terror, seemed to be out of control. I must have believed, at some level, that in order to survive I needed to be a "good," compliant child. Instead of obliterating important components of my real self, however, I channeled those energies into creating spunky, defiant, and brave puppet characters. In doing so, I survived my childhood and preserved, deep down, those healthy parts of myself. As an adult I learned, in the face of anger or fear, to be articulate and to stand up for myself. But even now—to my rather rueful amusement—there are times when I find myself more able to hold my own while speaking through Audrey Duck than without her.

During a break at an academic seminar recently, I approached a highly esteemed professor, whom I'll call Dr. Smith, to ask him a question and offer a dissenting opinion about his thoughts during the preceding discussion. He was someone who, in his world, was used to having his opinions count: what he thought *mattered* and was rarely questioned. We had been talking about the meaning of play, which—as you know by now—is something I care passionately about and have thought about a great deal. He dismissed out of hand my comments on the value of thinking about play as simultaneously real and not real. He didn't actually respond with the words "stupid idiot," but his manner was scornful enough that I actually started to feel under attack. To my chagrin, I grew less and less able to organize my thinking and was therefore unable to put forth a cogent argument for my point of view. The whole proceeding, which had been quite fun up to that point, no longer felt safe.

A few hours later, however, the seminar leaders asked me to demonstrate some of my work with puppets. Without conscious forethought by me, the following conversation ensued.

AUDREY: What are we doing here?
ME: We're here to talk about play.
AUDREY: What's play?
ME: You. You are play.
AUDREY: But am I real?
ME: Yes . . . and no.
AUDREY: You mean I'm not real?
ME: Yes . . . and no.
AUDREY: Gee. . . . What does Dr. Smith think?

Everyone in the room, including Dr. Smith, laughed when they heard that. I was pleased but also surprised at where the dialogue had taken me. It had been years since I'd felt the need to resort to Audrey's voice to say what I meant, or to respond to a challenge. But having that experience so recently has been useful. It reinforced in an immediate and personal way the amazing relationship between Audrey's voice and my "true" self. And it propelled me to think, once again, about the access that pretend play of all kinds provides to inner life. The time and space we allow for children to express themselves through pretend play provides them with tools that translate into adult coping skills—using any kind of creative medium as a means for self-expression and release.

If we perceive our environment as threatening or unsafe, we build façades to protect our sense of self from being wounded; meanwhile, the core of who we really are remains safely hidden behind the personae we create.

Most of us assume what Winnicott calls a "false self" on occasion, and being able to do so can be useful.[1] We "put our best foot forward" for job interviews. We tell "polite" lies to avoid hurting someone's feelings. We behave in a politic manner in meetings. We do what we need to do to function in society. But children growing up in environments that consistently deny or threaten the reality of who they are and what they feel are forced to maintain a false self most of the time. The costs are high. It takes a lot of psychic energy to build a wall—and to hold it up. In its more extreme manifestations, the ongoing need to maintain a false self can lead to depression or even suicide. With no outlet for emotional honesty, the danger is that we lose touch with who we really are and have no access to our own emotional truth.

Sometimes even the best intentions of parents and caretakers can result in transmitting a message to children that it is safer not to tell the truth. Children can be quite attuned to the emotional strengths and limits of the adults who love them and can easily pick up from us what we are and are not able to hear from them. When—for whatever reason—honest self-expression isn't a viable option for children, being able to use play to express their real feelings is an invaluable skill.

At four, Kara's strength shone through eyes bright with determination and resolve. Since graduating from her walker, she ricocheted through the day-care center like a little billiard ball. Her outstretched hands left faint prints on the center's walls, which provided her with support when she didn't want to use her crutches. She would never be able to count on her legs for balance. Sometimes she held my hand as we walked to and from our sessions, dragging me along impatiently to get wherever we were going.

Kara was born with HIV. She lived with her mother and father, who were also infected, and an older sister who was not. The virus has attacked Kara's central nervous system, which was why she had trouble walking. In addition to being on a rigorous regimen of medications, Kara had had major orthopedic surgery—twice. Her second operation occurred a few months after we first met.

Both of Kara's parents were positive, forward-looking, upbeat people. They didn't spend much time on grief; rather they devoted their limited resources to surviving and moving on. Given the amount of stress they had to cope with—poverty, Kara's HIV, her problems with her legs, and their own illnesses—their determination, strength, and optimism were remarkable and served them well.

In many ways, her parents' determination and their refusal to mourn served Kara well, too. If there were services to be had, Kara got them. If there were programs that would benefit her, she was in them. But, for Kara at least, there was also a cost to be paid for such an upbeat stance. At the age of four, she had learned to shoulder her fears and fantasies alone, even in the face of loss and trauma.

Kara's parents and teachers described her as "spunky," "tough," "aggressive," and, most of all, "controlling." The words "sad" or "scared" never came up. Her parents were sick. She was sick. She couldn't walk. She had to take vile-tasting medicine daily. Yet she was never seen as sad or frightened. Kara had learned early on that there was no room in her small and stressful world for any sign of weakness. Brief outbursts of rage were acceptable, even though they got her into trouble, but she was never allowed, even for a moment, to acknowledge or lay down her burden of grief and despair.

Kara struggled more than many children with medication. Perhaps because of her muscle weakness, she had a very difficult time learning to swallow pills. She gave Audrey medicine repeatedly, waving away her protests like flies.

"I don't like taking medicine," cried Audrey.

"Yes, you do," insisted Kara. "Her does like it," she said to me.

"No, I don't," Audrey cried again. But Kara would hear nothing of it. Not only did Audrey have to take her medicine, she had to *like* it as well. At an early age, children absorb their family's and society's norms about feelings and their expression. Kara believed not only that she had to take her vile-tasting medicine, but that she had to like taking it. Through Audrey I could at least provide an alternative point of view.

Kara's early puppet play with me was filled with death— parents dying, children dying. In fact, Kara's father had been terribly sick before the new "cocktail" drugs became available, and her parents had lost several friends and relatives to HIV. Death lurked beneath Kara's play like some sinister sea creature. It thrust abruptly through her fantasies, breaking through a surface of serenity to swallow unsuspecting family and friends. Unlike the children at the Corner Co-op, whose play about death was fanciful and generalized, Kara's play repeatedly involved specifics about the loss of people she loved and indicated a familiarity with the process and its attendant rituals.

In our second session, Kara pretended that Audrey's father gave her a congratulatory hug for taking her medicine. Suddenly she plucked the father off her hand and laid it down on the table.

KARA: Your dad died.
AUDREY: He died?
KARA: Yeah.
AUDREY: Guess how I feel about that?
Kara is silent.
ME: How do you think she feels about that?
Kara is silent. Ignoring our questions, she puts on another puppet.
AUDREY: Wait a minute. My dad died!
KARA: Yeah.
AUDREY: I feel sad.
KARA (*sadly*): Here's flowers for him.

A few minutes later, Kara introduced Audrey's mother and a baby, both of whom died almost as soon as they appeared. "Who's going to take care of me?" asked Audrey amid her tears. "I am," said Kara brightly. After that, during our sessions together Kara routinely killed off puppet characters.

When told of her impending surgery, the sparkle in Kara's eyes began to dim. Her medical play became more intense. One day she decided that Audrey had to go to the hospital and that she needed to be given her medicine intravenously—through a tube inserted into Audrey's "arm." She refused to answer any of Audrey's questions about why she was going to the hospital, or about why she needed an IV. It was up to me to step in and provide some information.

"But why am I going to the hospital?" Audrey asked again. When Kara didn't answer, I replied, "You go to the hospital if you're sick or if there is something not working right in your body that needs special care in order to get well."

Kara ignored my explanation. Because so many children at the center had lots of medical treatments, there was usually a doctor's kit filled with toy medical equipment in the office I used. Kara reached for a syringe to make Audrey have an IV and announced that Audrey was going to cry about it. On cue, Audrey began to cry.

AUDREY: Ouch. That hurts. I don't like it. I know I need it but I
    don't like it. I know it's going to help but I don't like this.
KARA: What are you gonna do?
AUDREY: Well, do I have to have this done?
KARA: Yeah.
AUDREY: Can I tell someone how I feel about this?
KARA: You can't tell your mom.
AUDREY: I can't tell my mom? Why not?
KARA: Because it's a secret.
AUDREY: Oh, no! Who can I tell?
KARA (*ignoring Audrey*): Breathe.
She has a stethoscope and instructs Audrey to take a deep breath.
AUDREY: Why can't I tell my mom?
KARA: It's a secret.
AUDREY: Why? Who told me to keep it a secret?

Kara seemed unsure about how to respond to this. And when Audrey pressed her for an answer about who said she had to keep her feelings a secret, Kara wouldn't or couldn't answer.

While anger, fear, and grief are perfectly reasonable responses to stress in the lives of children—from hospitalization to divorce to any kind of family strife—we often inadvertently put a lot of pressure on children not to share those feelings.

As a parent myself, I understand. When my daughter is unhappy, angry, or scared, I find her negative feelings sometimes harder to bear than my own. Built into the role of parent is a desire for our children to be well and happy. But it's essential to recognize and understand that this can't always be the case— and that there are situations where the expression of the emotions such as sadness, fear, or anger are not just appropriate but an indication of health.

For some of us, hearing our children openly express any kind of negativity is particularly difficult. Perhaps we have grown up in families where expressions of such feelings were not encouraged or were even actively discouraged; at the extreme, the culture of some families dictates that it's morally wrong even to experience negative feelings in the first place. These are preconditions that may lead a child to develop a false self that obliterates the true one, with crippling psychological effects. When children are seen in therapy over time, however, and have motivated parents who are (1) willing to do the psychological work necessary to change deep-seated habits and behaviors, (2) have the resources for long-term therapeutic work, and (3) are involved with agencies that have the resources to provide staff to *do* the work, then it's possible to effect positive change.

Unfortunately, those conditions don't always, or even usually, exist. Most of the children I've met in my work have been confined to the hospital for short-term stays and sent home without psychological support services, or are enrolled in daycare centers with minimal resources for family support. Many are from families living in poverty whose day-to-day struggle for survival consumes most of their emotional resources. I have great admiration for the staff and the families with whom I've worked. The reality is that without adequate supports, sometimes the best we can do is work for social change—and, in the meantime, provide children alternative models for coping. Kara's perception was that her mom was not going to be able to bear her fear and anger. The staff was going to be able to work with Kara's mom to help her accept Kara's fear and anger about the surgery, even as she was grappling with her own. But that was going to take time. Meanwhile, I wanted Kara to know that there were other people who could tolerate her feelings.

AUDREY: But can I tell somebody how I feel about being in the hospital? Who can I tell?

KARA: You can't tell your mom.

AUDREY: Can I tell my teachers at school?

KARA: No.

AUDREY: Can I tell Geneva [the school psychologist]?

KARA: No.

AUDREY: Can I tell Susan?

KARA: No!

Kara pretends to hurt Audrey by plucking at where her eyebrow would be if she had an eyebrow.

KARA: Pluck!

AUDREY: Owww! You plucked my eyebrow. I don't like that. Oww! That hurts! (*She sounds discouraged.*) Boy, I'm lying here in the hospital 'cause I need to get something fixed in my body and I don't like it and I can't even tell anyone. What would my mom do if I told her?

KARA: You can't tell her. (*She hurts Audrey again.*)

ME: There needs to be somebody who Audrey can tell how she feels. Because it's a big secret to keep. All these feelings! How do you think she's feeling about being in the hospital?

KARA: Her *has* to stay in the hospital.

ME: She has to stay in the hospital?

KARA: Yeah.

ME: And how do you think she feels about that?

Kara is unable to answer.

AUDREY: I'll tell you how *I* feel about it. I feel mad and sad and scared.

KARA: You do?

AUDREY: Can't I tell someone that?

KARA: No.

AUDREY: Why not?

Once more, Kara is unable to respond.

AUDREY: Am I gonna get better if I'm here?

KARA: No.

AUDREY (*shocked and dismayed*): No? Oh no! I want to tell someone. (*To me*) Can I tell Kara how I feel?

KARA: No.

AUDREY: Nobody?

ME: That's a big secret for a little girl to be carrying around.

At this point, Kara became very busy taking Audrey's blood and seemed to be ignoring everything I said. "I bet if you told your teachers in school," I told her, "they would understand how you feel about being in the hospital. 'Cause you know what? No one likes to be in the hospital." No matter how much Audrey argued, Kara refused to acknowledge the validity of any feelings Audrey expressed that day—but Audrey kept right on expressing them and I kept supporting her.

As Kara's hospitalization got closer, her eyes grew dull, as though she were viewing the world through a shroud. She never laughed, rarely even smiled, and she played with none of her characteristic joy or spunkiness. Instead, her interactions

with the puppets seemed propelled by compulsion, seething
with barely repressed fear and rage. She stumbled through her
fantasies, retracting only the most terrifying as they bubbled
forth. Yet she never wanted to stop. And even through her night-
mare images of abandonment—even as she condemned her
playthings to death and worse—I saw unmistakable glimpses of
her basic sweetness and the rock-solid reality that she was loved.

One day, when we were playing with both Audrey and Cat-
a-lion, she announced that Audrey had a doctor's appointment
and wasn't coming back. She let that horrifying possibility linger
for a moment before quickly changing her mind. Audrey would
return. Then Kara noticed a Band-Aid on Audrey's arm, a relic
of some other child's fantasy. She peeled it off and kissed Audrey. "You got a shot?" she asked tenderly.

"Does someone kiss you when you get a shot?" Audrey
asked. Kara nodded. "It hurts," she said. "I go to the hospital, I
get a shot."

Suddenly, Kara began to hit Cat-a-lion.

"Are you mad?" asked Cat-a-lion. "Yes!" answered Kara and
proceeded to hit Audrey. "Them don't like me!" she said to me.
"Are you mad at *them*?" I asked. "Can you use words to tell
them that you're mad? It's okay to be mad, but you can't hit."
"I'm mad at you!" Kara yelled. She said that Audrey was mad
too, but she didn't want Audrey to say why. Finally, Audrey
came out with it anyway: "I'm mad 'cause I have to go to the
hospital." Kara responded instantly and with loud enthusiasm:
"Yes! Yes! Yes!" But she refused to let Audrey elaborate.

Instead, she began busily nurturing a baby doll. She decided that the baby was going to the hospital. When I tried to
tell Kara about what happens when you have an operation, she
got even busier with the baby and appeared not to be listening,

but whenever I stopped she commanded me to continue telling Audrey about it.

Suddenly Kara decided that the baby needed to be locked up someplace with no one to take care of her. Then she announced that Audrey's mom couldn't come to the hospital—that she didn't even *want* to come.

In fact, because we'd talked about it, I knew that Kara's mother would be at the hospital as much as was humanly possible. It's important to remember that, because it emanates from inner experience, children's play may reflect their fears and fantasies rather than actuality—or some combination of the two. This was important information to share with her mom, who could reassure Kara as her hospitalization approached that she would not be abandoned.

As soon as Kara revealed her worst fears—that she would be abandoned—she decided to stop playing with puppets for a while and began to build with blocks. When it comes to grappling with inner life, pretend play has a built-in safety valve. Children usually stop a line of play when it ceases to be fun or becomes too threatening and, like Kara, move on to something else. Forced, or mandatory, play is an oxymoron.

I helped Kara with her block construction for a while, but soon she picked up another puppet and said that it was a baby. "Sometimes I feel like a baby," Audrey said. "You *are* a baby," proclaimed Kara.

Concerned that Kara needed reassurance about her fears of abandonment, I told Audrey that she could ask her mom whether she was going to be in the hospital with her. Kara's response was immediate and intense:

KARA: No you can't!!!!!
AUDREY: I can't?

KARA: No! No! No!
AUDREY: I'm mad!!!!!
KARA: No! No! No!

Audrey asked Kara one more time if *she* was mad. "Yes!" answered Kara. But she couldn't or wouldn't say why. Audrey and I, however, aren't quitters.

"I'm mad!" Audrey announced yet again. "No, you aren't," said Kara. When I suggested that Audrey really needed to tell her mom about her feelings and her fears, Kara remained firm in her commitment to secrecy: "No, her don't."

Audrey asked if we were going to see Kara again. When I said that we were, Kara announced that she was not coming back to her school again—she was going to the doctor and she wasn't coming back.

"That's what I'm scared of!" Audrey said. Kara reiterated that she was not coming back and her play got more intense. She pretended to cut her dolls and announced that they had died. Then she said that Audrey had died.

Kara's experience of her world, complicated by her terrible medical problems, dictated that she could not directly acknowledge weakness, fear, or rage. It was only in make believe that she could safely express these "unacceptable" emotions, so she used it to give voice to them, strongly and unmistakably. That she could do so is a tribute to her inner strength.

The next time I saw her, Kara wanted to feed the baby doll and insisted that Audrey had to be quiet: no talking because it would disturb the baby. Every time Audrey opened her mouth, Kara shushed her. She gave the baby a shot, but wouldn't let Audrey comment on it.

Because Kara's hospitalization was imminent, I pretended that Audrey was also going into the hospital soon. Audrey announced that she didn't want to talk about it, but Kara insisted that she had to.

"Do you think I have lots of feelings?" Audrey wondered. Kara nodded. But when Audrey asked what kind of feelings Kara thought she might have, Kara didn't answer. Audrey asked, "Why am I going to the hospital?" "Because you want to," Kara answered matter-of-factly. "I'm going to the hospital," she added.

I explained once again that although Audrey had to go to the hospital, she didn't have to *want* to go. Audrey asked what was going to happen to her there. "Shots," Kara explained and demonstrated by giving Audrey a needle. Audrey yelled and Kara stuck a bottle in Audrey's mouth. I continued to try to talk with Audrey about the hospital, but Kara changed the subject. Audrey asked why Kara needed an operation and Kara ignored that question too.

Audrey asked if her own mother could be with her when she herself went to the hospital. Kara's response was "No" but I chimed in rather loudly, "Yes!"

Then she decided that the baby doll needed an operation. Audrey wondered if the baby needed it because she was bad. Kara enthusiastically agreed. I intervened, explaining that operations have nothing to do with whether someone is bad or good.

For better or worse, preschool children tend to experience themselves not just as the center of the universe, but as the cause of events both major and minor. Part of growing up is relinquishing one's status as the sun around which the world revolves. We learn that other people have a point of view. We learn, more or less, that there are some things we control and some things over which we have no control at all. For children whose lives are filled with mostly good things this egocentricity is useful. It extends their early experience of being able to affect the world positively.

The problem is that when young children encounter tragedies large and small—death, divorce, hospitalization, moving, parental absences, family strife—they tend to see themselves as having caused these events as well. When I work with preschool children facing a crisis, my puppets always raise the issue of fault. "Is it 'cause I was bad?" Audrey will wonder. More often than not, young children will answer with a resounding "Yes!" It's up to me to reassure my puppets, and the children, that it's not their fault.

Pretending to be a doctor, Kara began to operate on the baby. In the middle of the surgery she said, "They're going to cut my legs open. It won't hurt." We talked about the anesthesia she would be getting.

In a few minutes, Kara's play became more dreamlike. Images laced together by themes of surgery, death, loss, and anger appeared and disappeared, shifting rapidly, overlapping, making no logical sense. She was creating a kaleidoscope of terror. Audrey's mom and dad died. Audrey died during her operation, killed by medicine she got in the hospital. Audrey died and became a monster. Her mom and dad died again. Audrey died again during her operation. Audrey was going to bite me. Kara woke Audrey up. She said that Audrey was dying from the medicine.

I reassured Audrey that she was not going to die from medicine. Kara got very busy with the baby doll and once again seemed not to be listening. She found some masking tape and began to tape up the baby. "Oh, it's like a cast," Audrey said. Kara continued to tape the baby with an urgency that almost seemed compulsive. She did not just tape the baby's legs, she

taped up everything as though she was wrapping a mummy—
hands, eyes, even the baby's mouth. She did not stop until the
baby was completely encased.

Then Kara explained that the baby needed a cast because
she fell and hurt herself. She said that the baby couldn't move.
It couldn't talk. It couldn't even sniff.

"I'm scared that I'm going to be taped all together in the
hospital," whimpered Audrey. "You will!" said Kara brightly. I
disagreed. I assured Audrey that she would not be in a cast forever. And it would start at her chest and encase her legs; it
would not cover her head and arms. Kara began wrapping herself in tape. Then she taped herself and the baby together. "The
baby won't have to be alone," I commented. Kara agreed. A few
days later, Kara went into the hospital. Contrary to her fears,
she came through her surgery well, and her mother and her
large extended family were all able to be there with her.

Interactive puppet play lends itself marvelously well to sorting through and integrating any dichotomies between inner
experience and outer expression. It's not the only medium
through which to do that—children's drawings, for example,
can also reflect an inner experience that's at odds with their
outer persona—but puppet play is particularly rich in possibilities. Unlike in a painting or a drawing, the viewpoint expressed
is verbal, which makes it relatively easy to decipher. In addition, as an expressive medium, puppet play is like cubism in
that it enables the simultaneous expression of many points of
view. This capacity to hold multiple dimensions, allowing for
ambivalence and ambiguity, is an incredibly powerful therapeutic tool.

When a child and I play with puppets, we can have as many
as six "people" in the room at the same time, each with a potentially different point of view. If we each bring ourselves and a

puppet to the play, there are four personae interacting. If we each add another puppet, there are six. If the children shift characters, as they often do, there are even more points of view to contend with.

At the same time, these characters (or the potential for these characters) serve as protective screens for unacceptable thoughts or feelings. Psychologically hidden behind a puppet, children can create a vengeful, raging monster, for instance, or a sadistic doctor, even as they present themselves as calm, even stoical, beings. The impulse for honest expression and the sense that a puppet's "separate" personality is a safe haven for that expression occur together spontaneously, instantaneously, and often without conscious realization.

The intricacies and subtleties of make believe are present whenever children play, whether they are alone, with other children, or in the presence of adults. When we are engaged in children's make believe, however, our responses can powerfully influence how or whether particular themes are elaborated upon. The sense of safety provided by pretend play is fragile. As with any therapeutic encounter, this safety depends on a shared understanding of and adherence to rules and boundaries. For instance, the children and I agree to play with puppets. What emerges through a puppet's voice is treated as fantasy. I almost never ask children to make connections between their own situations and the stories they create through play, although they are free to do so on their own. Any violence occurring during our sessions has to be fantasy. Neither I nor the children nor the puppets may be actually harmed. But the children and I are both free to say whatever we choose through the puppets.

These rules, except for the one about violence, need not be stated explicitly. Most of them are the rules children seem to employ naturally for any kind of shared expressive play. When Kara made Audrey's father die, I let her do it; however, even though she obviously wanted to let his death go by without comment, I was free to use Audrey to express feelings about it. Because we were "only playing," Kara was free to kill Audrey off in surgery, make Audrey's parents die, or leave her in the hospital forever.

Just as the children, as themselves, remain in the room when we play with puppets, I retain my own voice, separate from Audrey's. I am myself, in my role as a caring adult and therapist in the child's life. I am also Audrey's caretaker, although I do not define myself as her mother unless a child designates that role for me.

As with Kara I often use my own voice to validate children's feelings and to nurture their right to express them. I also defend Audrey's right to expressions of loss, fear, and anger—and the validity of those feelings. "It's okay to cry," I might say, or, "Anyone would be mad if they had to have an operation." Repeatedly, in as many ways as I can, I reassure children that, at least in our relationship, it is safe for them to be themselves.

My responses to the children's puppet characters and their expressions of feelings are key to this sense of safety and so are carefully considered. A child who makes a dragon puppet roar fiercely after Audrey Duck finds that there are no negative real-life repercussions. Instead my puppets respond with fear or sadness, and in my own voice or theirs I try to find a name for the feeling expressed by the raging dragon ("Are you angry?") and for the feelings that this rage may engender or be fueled by ("I'm scared!" "I'm sad!").

When Kara first made Audrey's father die and could not or

would not assign any feelings to Audrey in response to that trauma, I began to focus my efforts on helping her find language and space for expressing her own feelings. Much of the time, questions like "Guess how Audrey feels about . . ." are successful invitations to children for expression of their own feelings by proxy. Audrey usually owns whatever feelings the children assign her unless the feelings named are outrageously out of sync with the events (and they rarely are). If, for instance, a child says Audrey is happy that her father died, Audrey might respond, "Why would I feel happy?"

Seeing that Kara made no response to questions about Audrey's feelings, I decided that whatever the reason for her own silence it was important for Audrey to say that *she* was sad. In doing so, I accomplished several things simultaneously. Kara got to hear the word "sad" in connection with feelings about a death; she got to experience a "child" safely expressing sadness in the presence of an adult with no negative consequences.

Kara also needed a name for anger. Intense feelings of rage can be simultaneously so overwhelming and energizing that they can be hard to contain, especially for young children, whose capacity for self-control is still developing. Being able to recognize anger and name it is one step toward being able to manage it. Eventually Kara was able to recognize and even to acknowledge that she was angry. But then, as she was hitting Audrey, she made the seemingly puzzling statement that the puppets didn't like her.

My understanding of this statement is that Kara's rage was so intense and so frightening to her that she had to disown most of it. Instead of acknowledging her own feelings, she saw her rage reflected in those around her—even when it wasn't there. It's like the process that the analyst Melanie Klein called "persecutory anxiety." When our feelings are too overwhelming to bear, we sometimes separate ourselves from them, attributing them to others instead. In doing so, we may be temporarily relieved of feeling them, but then we might also experience the negative feelings as directed *at* us from the outside, rather than as coming from inside of us and being directed outward. This phenomenon can lead to some peculiar situations with very verbal toddlers.

"When you're angry you hit me!" a little girl announced to her astonished mother, who had never, ever, laid a hand on her. Another friend, who had also never hit her child, had the embarrassing experience of having her two-year-old, in a very public, very angry meltdown, passionately howl, "Don't hit me! Don't hit me!" As much as I sympathized with Kara's rage, I couldn't let her hit my puppets, so I encouraged her to use words instead. Once she was able to yell out her anger I could build on that by having Audrey announce, in ringing endorsement of Kara's feelings, that she was angry because she had to go into the hospital. Kara's "Yes! Yes! Yes!" was a real leap forward for a child who had previously been unable to name, let alone acknowledge or begin to understand, her difficult and very real feelings.

Kara's situation was extreme, but children growing up in easier, less stressful circumstances also experience powerful emotions in the normal course of their lives, emotions that can be disconcerting for the adults around them, even when expressed in play—as was the case with Megan, the little girl I described in Chapter 4 who threw her baby doll across the room upon hearing about the new baby who would soon be joining her family. In my experience, the emotions children express in their play may be fleeting, but chances are that they're real. Allowing them the freedom to use pretend play as a conduit for honest feelings—even those that we wish they didn't have—is an important way of validating their experience and allowing them to be themselves.

8

Angelo

Playing About Secrets

For a puppet, Audrey Duck has led a rather tormented exis-tence. At the hands of children she has contracted myriad life-threatening diseases and been cut up in a million pieces to be served to a team of doctors. She's undergone surgery with no anesthesia, been ravaged by monsters in front of her uncon-scious mother, and been abandoned in a hospital for twenty years with only one mean nurse.

Like any play therapist, I am acutely aware that children are capable of passionate rage and exquisite terror that may be manifest in explicitly grisly fantasy play. The horrors children concoct for my puppets are neither random nor accidental. The diseases Audrey has contracted are usually similar in symptoms and treatment to those experienced by the children who create them. The predicaments they invent for her often turn out to be metaphors for their own experience.

The little girl who cut her up and served her to doctors had undergone a year of numerous surgeries in a desperate attempt to save her life. The boy whose monster puppet attacked Au-drey while her mother languished unconscious had been severely abused by his father. He made Audrey's mom wake up each time the attack ended, upbeat, cheerful, and refusing to believe her description of the attacks. The child who abandoned Audrey in the hospital for years was in the throes of coping with a hospitalization of indeterminate length. Most of the children whose play I've described so far have inflicted some kind of violent torment on the characters created in our play together.

The need to play out upsetting, violent, or gruesome scenes is not relegated to children experiencing trauma. Hard as we try, we can't completely protect children from experiencing or witnessing some form of pain, suffering, conflict, or loss. Children feel pain when they fall and hurt themselves, or visit the doctor for injections, or contract ear infections. Grandparents die, as do beloved pets or family friends and acquaintances.

The darker side of childhood—that enthusiastic embrace of gruesome and violent fantasy often so shocking to adults—can emerge even in the play of children whose life experiences are relatively trauma-free. It's a way of gaining a sense of mastery over feeling small and helpless in a large, confusing, and sometimes frightening world. "Tell me a story that's scary," says three-year-old Sofia. "But not *too* scary." At almost four she says, "Let's pretend that you're a burglar and you want to steal my shoes."

One way children learn to cope with fear is to construct fantasy worlds in which they conquer all kinds of adversities. Some children, like Sofia, may want to play about surviving the frightening experiences they imagine. Being able to survive imaginary attacks from monsters, giants, or burglars of their own making allows children to gain a sense of themselves as competent, and to learn to cope with feelings of fear in manageable doses.[1] Others may master the anxieties and frustra-

tions of feeling small in a big world by pretending to be monsters that can conquer the most powerful people in their lives.
Five-year-old Scotty, for instance, loves to transform himself
into a huge, scary *Tyrannosaurus rex* and laughs hysterically
when his dad pretends to cower in fear as the giant dinosaur
approaches.

One four-year-old, hospitalized for a rather minor operation, expressed the complexity of his feelings about it by creating a threatening lion puppet as he was recuperating from
surgery. Over and over again he made the lion puppet roar furi-
ously after my puppets. "Why is that lion roaring?" I asked.
"He's mad," said Timmy briefly. "Oh," I answered, "I wonder
why." "He used to be king of beasts, and now he's not king of
beasts anymore," he replied. "Oh," I said again. "Will he ever be
king of beasts again?" "No," said Timmy sorrowfully. "Now he's
the last beast." He didn't have the words to say directly, "I'm fu-
rious and I feel so diminished by this experience." Or even: "I
used to feel good and now I feel lousy." But through his play he
was able to create a metaphor that absolutely captured those
feelings.

Sometimes the very measures we take to protect children
from real-life trauma actually engender profound confusion and
powerful, scary feelings that they can express only in their play.

Angelo was an eight-year-old child living with HIV whose
mother died of the disease and whose family was desperately
determined to protect him from that knowledge. Like Kara and
Joey, Angelo's life circumstances were complicated and challenging. But all children experience some degree of anger, fear,
and bewilderment about the world in which they live. This is
not to minimize Angelo's pain, but to make the point that his
life circumstance doesn't make him all that different from the
children you know and love. Most children come up against

the limitations of what their caretakers can bear to tell them about an often unjust and unfair world.

All play needs to be safe. Allowing play that deals with violence does not mean allowing children ever actually to hurt anyone—or to create play in groups that makes other children uncomfortable. Boundaries and limits need to be established and adhered to, and the feelings and physical safety of everyone involved need to be respected. If one child's fantasy violence is too scary for a playmate, then we need to help them find other things to do together.

In allowing Angelo, and other children, to play out violent themes, I try to provide a context for the violence—to imbue the experience with feelings and validate verbal expressions of feelings such as outrage and grief as legitimate responses to violent acts. I try to help them solve constructively the difficult, and even impossible, situations they create for the puppets. Even if they refuse to accept the solutions proposed, I believe it is valuable for me to provide them with the experience of working with someone to find constructive resolutions to difficult challenges. I make sure that my puppets ask questions and try to grapple with whatever is thrown at them. In doing so, I hope to help them avoid giving in to a kind of chronic cynicism and despair that would sap meaning from their lives.

Angelo lived with his grandmother and, occasionally, an older brother in east Boston. A devout Italian Catholic, Angelo's grandmother loved him fiercely, fed him loads of pasta, and couldn't bear to tell him the truth. She shielded him from her own chronic illnesses and from his older brother's drug abuse. For three weeks after the fact, she could not bring herself to tell him that his mother was dead, a casualty of the AIDS epidemic. Nor could she face telling Angelo that he, too, was HIV positive. Without her permission, the staff of his after-school program were legally bound not to tell him either. Her decision is not uncommon. For parents struggling with guilt over the behaviors that led to their disease as well as the stigma associated with having it, the thought of telling their children the truth is overwhelming. They are afraid that their children will be ostracized at school, or that friends and family will desert them. Even parents who would like their children to know the truth may be afraid that they will not be able to keep it secret from landlords, employers, or other people with power over their lives.

Angelo was a bright, observant kid, but his grandmother clung steadfastly to the belief that he did not notice the tragedies permeating his life. For a long time, there was nothing I or any other staff member at the center could say to convince her otherwise—despite mounting evidence from his play with me and his behavior in class that he knew a lot more than she thought.

Children often know and understand much more about their lives than we think is possible. Sometimes our desire to protect children from harsh reality causes them much more pain than being told the truth and can manifest in outbursts of rage or, more passively, in deep depression. While children may maintain a pretense of ignorance, the truth of what they know or don't know about family secrets can often be found in their play.

Angelo's participation in the center's program, and especially in our mental health work together, had been predicated upon an agreement with his grandmother that, while we would not lie to Angelo, we could not initiate telling him what she didn't want him to know. In other words, if he asked outright whether or not he had HIV, we could tell him—but we were not allowed to bring it up ourselves.

Because the staff believed that Angelo was so much better off having an ongoing therapeutic relationship and a chance to play out his feelings and concerns, I agreed to see him under these conditions. But I also joined the staff in a long process of helping his grandmother tell him the truth about all sorts of difficult problems: his grandfather's drinking, his brother's overdose, her own medical problems. Each time one of these issues was brought to light, I mentioned to Angelo that if he had any questions about anything, I would be happy to try to answer them. If I didn't know the answer, I would find someone who did. "Not right now," he usually answered. And he would continue to play.

The children with whom I work often come from families struggling with poverty, and sometimes that poverty, debilitating in and of itself, is complicated by generations of alcoholism, depression, and abuse. This was the situation for Angelo's family, and for that reason I have enormous admiration for his grandmother, who worked very hard to care for him and reached out to provide him with access to the resources available to him. "I would die for Angelo," she said fiercely in one of our meetings. "And if anyone ever hurt him . . ." She left the sentence unfinished, but I got her meaning.

His grandmother's desire to protect Angelo, together with an ingrained and particular style of coping with stress, led her to shield him from the truth. The web of deception reflected in Angelo's play was spun from love and the best of intentions. The staff believed strongly that this deception was harmful to him, yet we were all bound to respect his grandmother's wishes about what we could and could not tell him.

Meanwhile, she and the staff conducted an ongoing conversation about telling him the truth. Slowly, over time, she made some concessions. She finally told him that her missing toe was

due to diabetes. When Angelo witnessed his brother's drug overdose, she initially said only that Mark was ill, but when I con-
tacted her after Angelo told me, spontaneously, that he thought
his brother was on drugs, she came in immediately and the
staff helped her talk with him about what had really happened.

But whenever the issue of his HIV status was raised, Angelo's grandmother dug in her heels about telling him the truth.
"I'm not going to tell him until I absolutely have to," she repeated. "When will that be?" we asked, and kept working with
her grandson.

From the first time I worked with him, Angelo's play was
rife with violence, death, loss, and deception. During that first
session, he banished my puppets to Antarctica. It was the cold-
est place on earth and they were sent there by an evil Santa
Claus. They had to call the good Santa Claus to get them back
home to Brazil. When they arrived home, Audrey asked who
they lived with. "We're kids," answered Angelo's lion puppet.
"And we live alone."

Suddenly Angelo made the lion puppet beat up a beaver
and kill him. "Oh, no!" I said. "I'm sad that Beaver died." "He's
going to the hospital," Angelo announced. "They'll make him
better there." "But if you're dead, a hospital can't make you better," I commented. "He's just hurt," Angelo interrupted. "He'll
be in the hospital for eight weeks." "But where are Lion's and
Beaver's mom and dad?" I asked. "They used to live with their
mom," replied Angelo, "but they left because she wouldn't give
them a PlayStation even after they cleaned their room." "She
lied," said Angelo's lion puppet. "I *hate* people who lie about
having a PlayStation."

Angelo's comment is a great example of the rich complexity
of real-life experiences children bring to their play—like the
layers of a dream. This interchange could be reflecting simulta-

neously his confusion about his mother's death, feelings of abandonment, and deprivation—not to mention his longing for a PlayStation. Because we don't always know how literally we should take the details of children's play, I find myself often paying more attention to the themes that emerge rather than the literal content. In this case, the two themes I could identify were concerns about death and lying—specifically about being lied to.

The next time I saw Angelo he sent the puppets away again, this time to Africa, where the elephant puppet got badly injured. "He might . . . he might die," Angelo explained. He transformed the room into a hospital, using lots and lots of medical equipment to try to save the elephant. Before revealing the elephant's fate, Angelo announced that the puppet's grandma had gone to the hospital and died. "Oh no!" I exclaimed. "April Fools," he immediately responded. "She's really fine."

But ten minutes later, Angelo made all of his puppets die. Suddenly all of his puppets were alive again and involved in a rather chaotic brawl. Then he pretended that a goat bit Audrey and killed her and then she was miraculously brought back to life. Next, all of the puppets got shots. "What are the shots for?" I asked. "It's poison blood," Angelo answered excitedly. Needless to say, the puppets all died—again.

These sessions, among the first I had with Angelo, established the tangled themes of lying, medical treatments, death, and loss of a parent recurring in his play. Most poignant, given his diagnosis, was the image of the puppets getting shots of "bad blood." Hints that Angelo really knew the truth about his HIV status continued throughout our sessions. He infected Audrey with "the virus," and once announced that all of his puppets had an illness called "SRV." Week after week, Angelo's play depicted life as a violent and complex web of deception, full of contradictions and reversals. In Angelo's play, puppets were rendered unable to grieve, express outrage, or even get help. The outrages heaped upon them were often followed by voicelessness. One day, for instance, a lamb got shot and died. Angelo began marching around chanting, "Susan is dead. Angelo is dead." "Oh no!" cried Audrey. "This is awful." "Stop talking!" Angelo roared. "You can't talk. You can't talk about Lamb." No matter how much Audrey tried to talk, Angelo wouldn't let her utter a word. "Gee," I said, "it's hard having someone really sick or having someone die and not be able to talk about it."

In his efforts to pretend that Audrey was unable to talk, Angelo decided to deprive Audrey of her tongue. "You were born with the wrong tongue," he explained. "You need a new one." He insisted that she had to have a tongue transplant or she would not be able to talk when she was eighteen. But the doctor gave her the wrong tongue. She couldn't speak in her own voice and had to talk like Cat-a-lion. When I tried to make Audrey speak in her own voice, Angelo insisted that she could no longer speak at all—a poignant metaphor for the false self played out by Kara in the previous chapter. The only voice available to Audrey is one that doesn't belong to her. Over time, the theme of voicelessness continued to be a steady and expanding presence in Angelo's play as he created puppet after puppet who had difficulty talking.

One day he created a lamb who wanted to ask for help, but whose tongue was stuck to the top of her mouth. The lamb got increasingly agitated as Angelo rejected all of the solutions Audrey and I proposed for helping her. Finally, the lamb began banging her head on the table.

AUDREY: Hey, what's going on? Are you angry?
LAMB (*growling*): Yes! I want you to help me right now.

AUDREY (*worried*): I'm trying to help.

LAMB: Help me!

AUDREY: What can I do?

LAMB (*in despair*): I don't know. Just get me something.

AUDREY: What kind of—how about some water?

LAMB: No, I want to stick out my tongue. Help me!

AUDREY: I don't know how.

LAMB (*increasingly agitated*): Help me!

AUDREY: Angelo, what should I do?

ANGELO: I don't know.

Next Angelo made the lamb turn to him and plead, "Help me!" But instead of helping, Angelo got angry, saying fiercely, "Don't talk to me like that." He began to pretend to hit the lamb, which was on his hand. For a moment I watched him on the one hand—literally—express deep feelings of weakness and helplessness while simultaneously—and literally once again—beating himself up for it.

I intervened, wanting him to hear that it was okay to ask for help. "Wait! She's asking for help," I said. "Why are you hitting her?" The lamb continued to call for help as Audrey and I tried to figure how to come to her aid. But Angelo kept rejecting anything that I offered.

I had the sense that if I didn't do something, our play was not going to move forward. Angelo had created a situation that certainly reflected his own: he desperately needed help in all sorts of ways that might not be forthcoming. I didn't want to deny his experience by insisting that the lamb could be helped, but I needed to offer Angelo the prospect of hope and an opportunity to understand what he was playing out, instead of just feeling it. At this point, one option was to step out of the play and make an explicit connection to reality ("When you play like this, I wonder if you're feeling like the lamb"). Instead, I chose, as I usually do, to keep playing. I felt that Angelo had a lot more to say that he might only be able to express through his puppet play.

I made Audrey begin to cry and say, "It's scary. The lamb wants help and we *can't* help!" By keeping the focus on Lamb, without forcing Angelo to own feelings he might not be ready to admit, I hoped to provide him with information I thought he needed and to allow him to continue playing without inhibition.

"Help me!" Angelo made the lamb say once more.

"This is scary," Audrey said. "You want us to help you and we can't!"

Then the lamb's voice became much more powerful. "You see these people right here?" the puppet asked. "They didn't help me." Then, with rage, "I smashed them in the shape of an egg!" "Boy," I said to the lamb. "You are so angry at the people who didn't help you!" Lamb cried for help again, "Help me! Give me all the medicine that you have." I handed Lamb some medicine.

Two important things happened in this exchange. The lamb began to express anger instead of passive helplessness and I was able to identify that feeling for Angelo and connect it to the themes of help and hope. Once Audrey commented that the lamb was asking for help and not receiving it, Angelo was able to express anger and identify something that would actually help the lamb: medicine.

LAMB (*drinks the medicine*): It's poison!
ME: This is really tough. You think that the medicine I keep giving you is poisonous.
Angelo began to frantically pull instruments out of the doctor's bag.

ANGELO (*urgently*): Audrey, you check this stuff for unpoison-
  ing.
The lamb gets "unpoisoned" medicine.
ANGELO (*to the lamb*): Wow! Now, you're fine.

I continued to work with Angelo, even as he grew more interested in playing ball than playing puppets. The staff at the
center and I continued to help his grandmother move toward
disclosing the truth about his HIV status. Finally, with support
from the center's director, the nurse at the hospital clinic, and
myself, she was able to gather her courage and tell him the truth.

She, and he, were both hugely relieved. As I write this, it's
too soon to tell what bumps in the road Angelo will be facing
now that he knows his diagnosis. But at least now he is freed
from shouldering the burden of secrecy. He can ask for whatever help he needs, and we can check with him directly about
his fears and concerns. In our first session after Angelo learned
his diagnosis, he pretended that Audrey and Cat-a-lion both
developed HIV.

Play, or play therapy with or without puppets, cannot alter
the realities of chronic illness, poverty, death, or many other
threats to the well-being of children. What it can do is provide
children the freedom to express feelings, explore their experience of whatever life throws at them, help them gain a sense of
mastery instead of feeling helpless and overwhelmed, and provide the adults who love them with clues about how to help
them cope.

As I noted earlier, Angelo's life circumstances are extreme,
which is why he needed to engage in play with a therapist. But
being human is complicated for all children, and the complexities they meet up with are reflected in their play. They may
not need therapy, but they do deserve a chance to use make

believe—if they so choose—to marshal their inner resources toward coping successfully with whatever they encounter.

While it may be troubling to watch, the violence manifest when children channel inner conflict or external stress into their make believe play can be valuable if they can use it to confront fear, deal with their anger, or work on making meaning of overwhelming and confusing life issues. For adults, one major confounding factor in sorting out how to respond to violent play is that many children today, even those living in apparently safe and protected environments, encounter malicious intent and the mayhem it wreaks on a daily, or even hourly, basis.

Among the starkest changes electronic media have wrought in modern childhood is the degree to which children are immersed in images of graphic violence. Because we think of screen violence as merely entertainment, it's easy to dismiss its power. Because we are all so used to seeing people maimed, mutilated, and killed on television, in movies, or as part of video games—and because it's not "real"—it is easy to believe that media violence has no effect on children. But that's not the case. One especially powerful way to experience its impact is to look at the ways viewing screen violence affects how children play.

PART THREE

The Realities of Make Believe

Play and Cultural Values

9

Wham! Pow! Oof!

How Media Violence Is Killing Play

Five-year-old Sam stood feet apart, smack in the middle of his preschool classroom wielding his own genuine replica of a *Star Wars: Revenge of the Sith* electronic lightsaber. Gripping the handle with both hands and looking like the very model of a modern Jedi knight, he swooshed it around decisively, blocking attacks and vanquishing enemy aggressors—over and over again.

Fascinated by his perfect rendition of Anakin Skywalker in battle, I waited for Sam to make something else happen. But he didn't. Instead, enemy after imagined enemy met his doom in exactly the same way. Eventually, after he came perilously close to accidentally clobbering more than one of the children running past, his teacher drew him into another kind of play.

Revenge of the Sith is rated PG-13. Because of the film's explicitly violent scenes, the movie industry rated it as unsuitable for children twelve and under. Yet the manufacturer of Sam's lightsaber recommends it for children as young as four. Many of the blockbuster action films rated PG-13, from *Spiderman* and *The Incredible Hulk* to *Pirates of the Caribbean* and *Trans-*

formers, are promoted by marketing licensed toys to play out the violence seen on the screen. Of the 129 toys marketed with *Transformers*, 117 were rated as suitable for children five and younger.[1] Nor is Sam's rather mechanized rendition of a battle depicted on a screen unusual. Viewing violence on a screen seems to encourage imitation rather than creativity.[2]

The negative impact that screen violence can have on children's behavior and attitudes has been well documented elsewhere and is not the focus of this book, so I'll touch on it only briefly. In a review of one thousand studies conducted over thirty years of research, a consortium of the major American public health organizations concluded that "viewing entertainment violence can lead to increases in aggressive attitudes, values and behavior, particularly in children."[3]

There's no getting around the fact that electronic media and the marketing campaigns that sustain it have drastically increased the amount and kinds of violence to which children are exposed. Nor is film the only culprit. Nearly two out of three television programs contain some violence, averaging about six violent acts per hour.[4] By the time a child is eighteen years old, he or she will visually witness two hundred thousand acts of violence, including forty thousand murders on television alone.[5]

While there is no tally yet of the number of virtual murders or acts of maiming that children commit while playing video games, their game time is escalating.[6] According to market research, 46 percent of heavy video game users are between six and seventeen, and violent video games are quite popular with children.[7] The Grand Theft Auto series, where players can earn points, for instance, by having sex with a prostitute and then killing her, is a best seller among teens and preteens[8]—despite being rated M (for mature), which, according to the video game industry, means it "may be suitable for persons ages 17 and older."[9]

In a recent installment in the series, the M-rated *Grand Theft Auto: Vice City Stories*, players can kill off rival gang members, law enforcement officers, and innocent bystanders as they attempt to set up their own illicit businesses, such as drug dealing and committing armed robbery. I don't know how many very young children are playing games like this, but I do know that at one school where I have been working with the staff, most of the eight- and nine-year-old boys received a Grand Theft Auto video game for Christmas last year.

The interactive nature of video games—the fact that players can actually participate in virtual violence, rather than merely observing it, and that they are rewarded for committing acts of violence—raises a reasonable concern that they are even more apt to affect children's attitudes and behaviors than other kinds of screen violence. In fact, the U.S. Army has chosen to use popular violent video games—not television programs or films—to train their special operations forces for combat.[10] At the 2006 Summit on Video Games, Youth and Public Policy, academic, medical, and health experts signed a statement based on existing research saying: "Behavioral science research demonstrates that playing violent video games can increase the likelihood of aggressive behavior in children and youth."[11] An M rating does not seem to be an adequate deterrent. The Federal Trade Commission recently reported that 42 percent of unaccompanied thirteen- to sixteen-year-olds were able to purchase M-rated games.[12]

Meanwhile, there are few societal barriers to exposing children to violence on the screen. There's a dearth of regulation about what media programs can and cannot be marketed to children, so screen violence is readily available to them—on television, DVDs, video games, and now cell phones, MP3 players, and other handheld screen devices.

Experiencing brutality on the screen isn't the same as experiencing it in real life. But it's a mistake to dismiss the powerful effect it can have on children. Recent studies of the impact of media violence on the brain suggest that on some primitive, physiological level, we may not entirely differentiate between real-life violence and brutality on the screen. The use of magnetic resonance imaging (MRI) to assess the impact of media violence is in its early stages, but the results of these studies are intriguing.

According to Michael Rich, the pediatrician directing the Center for Media and Children's Health at Boston Children's Hospital, "The research suggests both that violent screen media content is processed differently than other screen content and that it seems to parallel the same patterns of brain activity as when survivors with post-traumatic stress disorder relive their traumas." This kind of research is beginning to provide neurological support for the behavioral studies demonstrating that children who watch a lot of media violence are triggered more easily to engage in violent behavior.[13]

Proponents of allowing purveyors of violent media more or less unfettered access to children claim that these products help children cope with their anger, fear, and aggression.[14] It can be cathartic, in that viewers can feel a release of emotion and may even feel better after watching violent media.[15] Catharsis in and of itself, however, doesn't contribute to a deeper understanding of ourselves and our behavior. Neither does it lead to finding constructive solutions for solving problems that may lead to violence. And if viewing media violence inhibits children's creative play, it is stifling activities that may promote effective problem solving and prevent violent behavior.[16]

Proponents also argue that viewing violence on a screen is simply an evolution of the age-old practice of telling children fairy tales, myths, or legends. But there are important differences—most obviously that written or oral stories afford children a significant amount of control over the visions they conjure while reading or listening. They can elaborately embroider scenarios or leave them vague, depending on their experience, predilections, and desires. But, other than shutting their eyes or having the maturity of judgment to remove themselves physically, they have no control when violent images wash over them from a screen.

Another difference between screen violence and violence on the printed page is that reading is dependent on a certain level of cognitive maturity. Inherent limits are set on the kinds of written content to which children have access without some kind of adult mediation because they have to learn to read, and that capacity develops over time. Access to print material depends on children's ability to read and their vocabulary, or on the availability of someone to read the story aloud. Stories told *to* children are completely dependent on their relationships with adults or older children. The necessity of adult presence heightens the possibility that children will be able to ask questions and talk through frightening or confusing material, and we can be proactive in initiating these conversations. It doesn't take much skill or cognitive maturity, however, to grasp explicit visual depictions of decapitations, eviscerations, dismemberments, or other kinds of mayhem. On a superficial level—just recognizing destruction when it occurs—screen violence is readily decoded.

Children's ability to grasp abstract concepts such as motivation, or complex psychological and social context, also develops over time. Meanwhile, advances in technology make it possible to depict in exquisite detail any manner of gore. In combination, these two phenomena render media violence simultaneously more meaningless and more compelling for young children. They don't understand why people are getting blown up or what motivates one person to throttle another, but they do tend to remember those moments—the most immediately exciting or dramatic action they see on a screen.

The power of screen violence combined with its inhibiting effect on creative play places children in a worrisome double bind. They may have intense responses to what they see on a screen. They may be confused, frightened, fascinated, or titillated by what they see. Yet something about that experience inhibits or otherwise disturbs their capacity to generate the kind of make believe play that's so useful for processing difficult experiences.

When the children I see in play therapy enact the same scene repeatedly with no variation, session after session, it can be a signal that there is some experience that has overwhelmed them. Julia, removed from her home for neglect, began our play sessions for weeks by creating scenarios featuring a mother who slept through her child's requests for food and help getting to school. Jennifer, a child the staff suspected of having been sexually abused, repeatedly put a puppet to bed and then blocked from my view what was happening to her.

When this kind of repetition occurs, I find that it may mean they are psychologically stuck in some way—something has happened that they can't make sense of or find a way to resolve. A frightening or incomprehensible event can manifest like a huge obstruction in the realm of children's fantasy life—like a chunk of something they ate that can't be digested—preventing the fluidity and growth that generally characterizes children's make believe.

Now, teachers of young children are reporting that same mechanized, repetitive play in children whose lives are saturated with media violence.[17] Marissa Clark, a preschool teacher, described to me an entire classroom of four-year-olds one year who were obsessed with superheroes. On the one hand, she understands the appeal. Preschoolers, in the throes of learning about right and wrong behavior, are fascinated by stories about good and evil. Surrounded by powerful adults or older siblings, and struggling with feelings of weakness or helplessness, the notion of magically transforming into an all-powerful being is irresistible.

What troubled Marissa is *how* the children were playing.

> I found that the children playing about media violence just followed the script of what they were seeing. It didn't really evolve and it just kept happening over and over and over again. I'd see a lot of kids holding their arms stretched out straight in a strong position, legs spread side to side and pointing at something and that would be Batman—he's got those gloves that are weapons. Other kids would be running and doing those high jump-kicks. Those were the Power Rangers. Others would be holding a hand palm up with their wrist sort of pointed down—they were Spiderman, casting his web. Once kids get into this kind of play, then all they do is the action. Then it can get really aggressive.[18]

Sometimes children imitating media violence get hurt in real life. After the ultraviolent World Wrestling Entertainment shows were introduced in Israel, researchers documented what they described as an epidemic of school-yard injuries caused by kids imitating wrestling moves.[19]

This is not to argue that children's media should be saccharine sweet or devoid of conflict. Nor does it mean that even eleven- or twelve-year-olds can't benefit—in the context of adult guidance—from viewing thoughtful films about the Holocaust, such as *Schindler's List*, or African genocide in *Hotel Rwanda*, or the marvelous television series *I'll Fly Away*, set in the American South during the struggle for civil rights, all of which feature violent themes. In fact, films like *Schindler's List*, which has powerful potential as an educational tool, come up frequently when I hear debates about media violence and children—usually as a reason for why advertising violent media to children should not be regulated. It's a specious argument. Unlike the *Transformers*, for instance, *Schindler's List* wasn't advertised during television programming for preschoolers on stations like Nickelodeon.[20] It didn't premiere in movie houses heralded by a host of Nazi action figures, Holocaust-themed junk food, and a promotional deal with Burger King. It wasn't marketed to children.

Because media violence today is so pervasive and graphic—and because so much of it is gratuitous, included merely to get people's attention or to sell products—I believe that it would be best, especially for young children, if we could find ways to limit their access. At the very least, we shouldn't be actively marketing media violence to them and we need to educate parents about its harms. We also have to help those children who are growing up unprotected from a culture saturated with media violence to cope with the images they see. Children need *safe and constructive* opportunities to work through their responses to whatever they're grappling with, whether it's in real life or in the media. If young children are exposed to media violence, it's likely that some form of what they are seeing will turn up in their play. It's also likely that they will need help finding ways to constructively play about it.

I've spoken with parents and teachers who prefer to limit all hints of play violence in their homes and classrooms. But I agree with child development specialists like Diane Levin and Nancy Carlsson-Paige, authors of *The War Play Dilemma*, who argue that our task is to allow children to play out in some way the violence they experience through the media, but that in doing so we have to help them move beyond endless imitation.

When I spoke to Diane Levin, she explained: "Adults struggle about how to deal with violent play. On the one hand, we know that children bring to their play what they need to work on—so we need to respect and value that. But on the other hand, we know that children learn from their play. When they are engaged in violence, we worry that they're going to be learning harmful lessons. And both sides are right. That's the war play dilemma."[21]

She pointed out that all violent play isn't the same. When it's rooted in media violence and when children's toys replicate exactly what they see on the screen, children get stuck in doing the same things repeatedly: their play doesn't evolve and is no longer a vehicle for meeting their needs or helping them understand the world. Levin says:

> When children are merely imitating, then they are much more likely to learn the harmful lessons that media teaches. But when they are involved in creative play that changes and evolves over time, it becomes less violent and more about problem solving. The power of the media images prevents them from being able to use play constructively—and some children never learn how to use it.[22]

Backed by billions of dollars, violence is sold to children through media characters designed and marketed to grab children where they are most vulnerable. It's not surprising that children love characters like Spiderman or the Power Rangers.

The capacity to transform from relatively weak to all-powerful taps deeply into feelings of inadequacy or powerlessness inherent in any developing child.

But media-based toys that promote violence are created for the sole purpose of turning a profit, not to promote creative play or any aspect of children's well-being. These characters pose particularly pernicious problems for parents and teachers concerned about children's welfare both because they are ubiquitous and because they exploit deep psychological needs. They can be encountered *everywhere*—on screens, in the grocery store, and even in some schools. It's true that children love them. It's also true that we have legitimate grounds to be concerned about their impact.

Children identify with raging against oppressors and can gain tremendous satisfaction from vanquishing opponents and triumphing over evil. They are also taught hour after hour, day after day, that violence is a legitimate—if not the only—solution to conflict. Ironically, they learn that lesson more powerfully when violence is presented as justified.[23]

When I compare descriptions of how children who are exposed to a great deal of media violence play to my own work with children who have encountered real-live trauma, the suggestion that our brains experience media violence in a manner similar to post-traumatic stress seems quite plausible. Without help, children engaged in play that imitates screen violence—characterized, for instance, by stylized martial arts or wrestling moves and verbalized sound effects ("Wham!" "Pow!" "Oof!")—either seem to stagnate in perpetual fantasy battle or devolve into an actual one. In that sense, their play is similar to that of children coping with actual trauma.

The ubiquity of violent media characters marketed as toys to preschoolers, such as Spiderman or Optimus Prime from

Transformers, and the lessons they teach are some of the reasons I believe that companies shouldn't be allowed to market directly to children and that children benefit when families can postpone exposure to commercial culture for as long as possible. If and when these bonds are forged, however, we need to find ways to acknowledge and validate children's fascination with these powerful superheroes without undermining their creative play. It's unfair to expose them to media programs designed to hook into their wishes, dreams, and fears and then deny them the opportunity to use play to work them through.

Allowing children to express their fascination with superheroes or other media through play does not mean that we need to buy into the products these programs sell. One parent whose seven-year-old son was devoted to Pokémon got so tired of the program, the repetitive violent play, and the pressure to buy all of its surrounding licensed products that she decided just to put an end to it. Once she refused—literally—to buy into the craze, her son decided to make his own Pokémon cards featuring his own made-up creatures. She found that after a while he and his friends were more interested in their own creations than the commercial version.

It often takes a lot of time and patience to help children break through the scripts they're imitating to what's really on their minds or what they're actually struggling with. In my role as a therapist, when the little boys—it's usually boys—who come into my office begin (always with the same sound effects) to randomly smash the dollhouse dolls or toy animals, I often try to bring feelings and context into their play. "Why is he doing that? Is he angry?" I might ask. "That's scary," I might add. Or even, "Boy, it sure must hurt if you get pushed off a roof." If I'm assigned the role of a child in the play session, I might voice how scary it is to watch people hurting each other.

For teachers or parents, one way to help children move beyond acting out the kind of repetitive, meaningless actions so often triggered by screen violence is to honor their delight in the characters they're portraying and help them play out other kinds of themes with them. Both Diane Levin and Nancy Carlsson-Paige suggest encouraging children to incorporate their interest in superheroes into creative art projects—like decorating their own superhero cape or drawing their own made-up superheroes. Can the Power Rangers build a house together, for instance? Another possibility is to switch media—can we paint about the Power Rangers? Can we fashion equipment for them made out of clay?

My interactions with Angelo, described in the previous chapter, took place in the context of a therapeutic relationship, but they remind me of the challenges posed for teachers and parents when children get stuck repeatedly imitating media violence. Instead of being rendered helpless by feelings of grief, confusion, and rage, all children need an opportunity to express those feelings safely and actively grapple with the circumstances in which they find themselves.

Repressing their impulses to play out violent themes isn't helpful. But it is equally unfair to leave them trapped in an imaginary cycle of violence. It's not my goal to impose resolutions on the fantasy situations children create when we play together, but rather to help them find their way through—and in the process enable them to experience themselves as powerful, competent, and creative human beings.

Getting stuck in repetitive, media-based violent play still tends to be a boy thing these days. But twenty-first-century little girls are also having their options for play constricted by media images reinforced by toys and accessories.

The Princess Trap

Make Believe and the Loss of Middle Childhood

"Let's play princess," four-year-old Abigail suggested. We were playing in the dress-up corner of her preschool, furnished with a battered old wooden sink and stove, a paint-splattered table, and a treasure trove of discarded adult finery. "Okay," I replied. "Which princess are you?" she asked. I was puzzled. Her question implied a set of particular princesses and was a less open-ended query than, "What's your name?" I glommed onto the first name that popped into my head. "Umm . . . I'm Princess Anna," I said. In a tone of amused exasperation, she responded instantly and authoritatively. "*That's* not a princess." "Really?" I asked, bewildered. She reeled off a list, including Belle, from *Beauty and the Beast*; Ariel, from *The Little Mermaid*; Aurora, from *Sleeping Beauty*; and the eponymous Cinderella—the main properties in the Walt Disney Company's stable of princess characters culled from animated movies based primarily on fairy tales.

When they are not being used as marketing tools, I have to admit that I love fairy tales. Populated with fantastical beings and abounding with wonder, they are terrific springboards for make believe. From the safety of "Once upon a time . . ." fairy tales allow children enough distance to grapple safely with the most passionate of human emotions—grief, envy, fear, rage, and joy. With plots simple enough for even young children to follow and enough twists and turns to stand up to retelling, fairy tales explore the trials of family strife and the human capacities for greed, loneliness, and courageous fortitude in the face of overwhelming odds.[1]

Fairy-tale plots tap into primordial themes: good triumphs over evil; the weak outwit the strong; cleverness outwits brawn; and—against seemingly impossible barriers and long struggle—virtue is rewarded. A happy ending is ensured—except, of course, in the stories made up by Hans Christian Andersen, like "The Little Match Girl," which I find almost too painful to bear.

Most of the stories we know of as fairy tales are hundreds of years old and had their origin as folk tales passed on through generations for amusement and education. All cultures have such stories, and many of them have similar themes. The roots of many of the most well known fairy tales lie in eastern and Middle Eastern folklore that made its way west during the Middle Ages.[2] It's ironic that Cinderella, currently imprinted by Disney in the national—and international—psyche as blonde and blue-eyed, is thought to have her origin in a ninth-century Chinese story called "Shen Teh." Disney based his animated film on a seventeenth-century version told by Charles Perrault, a Parisian intellectual who was spinning his stories for the French court.[3]

In Germany a century later, Jacob and Wilhelm Grimm also collected and retold old stories. The Grimm fairy tales are thought to be truer to the originals than Perrault's versions, and they can be quite gory. Because they describe explicit acts of violence, some people balk at reading the Grimm Brothers' versions to young children. In "Cinderella," the eldest stepsister obeys her mother's order to cut off her toe in order to fit the lost slipper. The youngest cuts off her heel. As retribution, their eyes are pecked out by doves.[4] In "Snow White," the Wicked Queen sends a hunter out into the forest with our heroine to kill her. Instead, he lets her go and slaughters a deer, bringing back its heart and liver as proof that Snow White is dead. The Queen promptly cooks them up and eats them. In the end, as punishment for her misdeeds, she is forced to don red-hot iron shoes in which she dances "until she dropped down dead."[5]

Fairy-tale violence shared with children in books or stories may certainly be hard for some of them, but it is not *nearly* equivalent to screen violence in its potential to terrify. When reading or listening to stories, children aren't assaulted with precreated graphic visual imagery. They don't have to see close-ups of a knife slicing through flesh or feet sizzling in an iron shoe, or the agony of pain in the queen's eyes as she dances to her death. Children have more control over how vividly they envision the violence.

I'm not, however, above skipping the torture scenes when I read these stories to kids. This is a personal predilection and not a philosophical stance. The specifics aren't really essential to the plot and always leave me queasy. Sword fights, an occasional giant slaying, or the rapid demise of wicked ogres don't bother me, but I tend to be haunted by even truncated descriptions of slow, painful death. Some people, including children, have a higher tolerance for that sort of thing. For some, the violence is just scary enough to serve as a springboard for playing about and safely exploring their own feelings of fear and anger.

"My four-year-old granddaughter loves the gruesome parts of Snow White," a grandmother tells me. "She likes me to put on my red bedroom slippers, dance wildly, and then fall down dead. We do that over and over." With older children, the violent punishments concocted in fairy tales can even serve as a springboard for talking about social issues such as justice, retribution, and torture.

Even aside from the violence, I suppose that my love of fairy tales rests uneasily on my social conscience. While their emotional content runs deep, the characters do not, and therein lies their biggest problem. There's no getting around the fact that they originated at a time when the roles of women and men were severely constricted, for instance, or that they often promise young girls a happily-ever-after in the form of marrying a handsome prince.

While I admit that I've tried on occasion to retell the stories from a more feminist slant—and have seen similar attempts in plays and puppet performances—they often fall flat and end up seeming like political tracts. One of the best retellings of a fairy tale from a more feminist perspective is the book *Ella Enchanted*, by Gail Carson Levine—but it's really more of a riff. Levine used the plot structure and characters to tell a more complex story in much the same way that Tom Stoppard elevates and expands the minor characters of *Hamlet* in the play *Rosencrantz and Guildenstern Are Dead* or the way Gregory Maguire humanizes the Wicked Witch of the West in his novel *Wicked*.

Speaking of wicked witches, the villains in fairy tales are especially one-dimensional. Bad characters are thoroughly bad, and with a few exceptions, like the Wicked Queen in "Snow White," thoroughly ugly. When children repeatedly receive the unchallenged message that physical traits reflect character flaws, we are training them to embrace societal stereotypes that are both wrong and deeply hurtful.

This came home most painfully to me when I was working

with an eight-year-old girl who had Aperts syndrome, a rare congenital disorder that results in facial deformities. Somehow the subject of play-acting came up. "I don't like it when kids want me to be in plays," she said passionately. "They always make me be the witch or the monster." She paused for a moment. "How would *you* like to always be the witch?"

By contrast, the heroines in fairy tales are as beautiful as they are good. As a child, I remember them often described as "fair of face," which can be read simultaneously as "nice to look at" and "light-complexioned." That beauty and a fair complexion are equated in these stories is not particularly surprising. Eighteenth- and nineteenth-century Europe was hardly a diverse or equitable society. Discrimination against the darker Semitic populations who were cordoned off in ghettos was common, as was the enslavement of Africans. That the stereotypes are explainable, however, does not eliminate the challenges fairy tales pose for those of us struggling to build a society that embraces similarities between people and celebrates the differences.

Because the stories are so rich, and because they lend themselves so well as springboards for make believe, I think that it's worth wrestling with fairy tales to allow them a place in children's lives. It's possible to find fairy tales that do feature strong women. Various versions of the same fairy tale portray women differently. Cinderella as characterized by the Grimm Brothers is significantly more resourceful than the Cinderella portrayed by Perrault.[6]

Race and gender are the most common stereotypes perpetuated in fairy tales, but there are others as well. As a child, I was particularly delighted that younger siblings were not only invariably good, but usually triumphant—often over their more powerful older siblings. I am, of course, a youngest sister. As an adult, I'm continually bothered by the ubiquitous characterization of stepmothers as wicked. "Not all stepmothers are bad," a five-year-old informs me. I'm glad someone thought to tell him—although "most stepmothers are good" might have pleased me more. (As you've probably guessed, I am a stepmother.)

If, as I do, you believe in the value of traditional fairy tales despite their flaws, then it's essential to share them thoughtfully with children, in the context of lots and lots of other stories featuring a whole range of cultures and characters. Since fairy tales originate in oral tradition and evolved to reflect particular cultures, I don't have a problem with editing a bit as I read or tell them to children. Giving heroines coal black hair and beautiful brown skin doesn't alter the plot or diminish the themes. There's no reason for Cinderella to be either blonde or white. The argument that we need to be true to the historical roots of these stories just doesn't make sense. If we were being really true to the historical roots of Cinderella, she would be Chinese.

When fairy tales become commercial megabrands, their depth and malleability diminish, and so does their value as springboards for creative play. Once fairy tales become visual versions of someone else's values—viewed over and over and sold to us in combination with tiaras, jewels, ball gowns, and castles and plastered with images of specific princesses with specific physiognomies—they lock children into a set script for playing from which it is very hard to deviate. Immersion in the Disney Princess brand—with its focus on glitter and acquisition—precludes playing out the more psychologically meaningful aspects of the stories that take place before the heroine becomes a princess: themes of loss, sibling rivalry, and parent-child conflicts.

A few minutes into playing with Abigail, the little girl who wanted me to be a Disney princess, she assigned me the task of scrubbing the floor. Looking up from my hands and knees I said brightly, "I must be Cinderella." "No!" she responded authoritatively. "You're Anastasia." I remembered that in the Disney version of "Cinderella" Anastasia is the tall skinny stepsister. "Anastasia never scrubbed a floor in her life!" I retorted rather scornfully. "She does in *Cinderella III*," Abigail replied sweetly. I stopped scrubbing. "There's a *Cinderella III*?" I asked in amazement. "Of course," she said, "after Cinderella is married."

Disney Princess retail sales reached $3.4 billion in 2006, with over forty thousand licensed items for sale.[7] I found 235 items on the Toys "R" Us Web site alone, including Disney Princess Monopoly; a Disney Princess Magical Talking Kitchen, with eleven phrases and eighteen accessories; Leapster Educational Disney Princess Enchanted Learning Set; and Disney Princess Uno. In addition to *Cinderella I, II,* and *III* on DVD, there's also *Disney Princess Stories* and *Disney Princess Sing Along Songs*, volumes 1, 2, and 3; Disney Game World: *The Disney Princess Edition*; *Disney Princess Party*, volumes 1 and 2; *Little Mermaid*, volumes 1 and 2; *Aladdin*, volumes 1, 2, and 3; *Beauty and the Beast* and *Beauty and the Beast: The Enchanted Christmas*.

The negative impact of Disney's presentation of women on little girls' conception of themselves and what it means to be female have been discussed in detail elsewhere.[8] Their ultrathin body types, their clothing, and the stories they tell embody a commercialized, stereotypic image of beauty and womanhood. More than ever before, Disney is having a profound effect on make believe. Like the superhero–action figure phenomenon, the Disney Princess films and their accoutrements trap children—little girls, this time—in an endless, intensifying loop of commercially constructed fantasies. Instead of pointing them toward violence, commercialized make believe for girls steers them toward a view of femininity based on stereotypes of beauty, race, class, and behavior. "I was shocked," a friend said, "when I saw my three-year-old niece reject a doll, saying, 'She can't be a princess, she's too fat!'"

"What's a princess?" I asked Abigail. "A rich girl," she answered promptly, "with a kingdom." She was a bit fuzzy on exactly what a kingdom is, however. "It's got lots of rooms," she explained tentatively. Then her eyes grew big and round, sparkling with excitement. "And now there's no food in it!" "Oh, no!" I groaned. "Yes!" she said with joyful urgency. "The servants have run out of ingredients!"

Once the royal trappings are removed from Abigail's play, it's hard to miss the values promulgated by the Disney brand, even aside from body image. The female ideal is a rich white girl who lives in a big house with servants who do the work. "I asked my three-year-old niece what she wanted to be when she grew up," sighed a colleague. "She said that she wanted to be a princess. She's totally into Disney."

Unless we make a special effort, Disney's animated version of fairy tales like "Cinderella" and the values they promote may be the only ones to which children are exposed. Disney is one of three multinational media corporations controlling most of children's commercial culture.[9] Its dominance, reinforced by an endless loop of toys, clothing, food, accessories, and media, is used to ensure that little girls buy into a lifestyle rooted in the things that Disney sells.

Newborn baby girls can come home from the hospital to be ensconced in a room decked out with princess furniture and paraphernalia. Videos, toys, accessories, and a longing to visit a Disney theme park will see them through childhood. Disney began selling wedding dresses in 2007,[10] but the company was hyping weddings long before that. A 2003 commercial for the Princess dolls features wedding dresses for Belle, Aurora, and Cinderella.[11] Brand-loyal little girls can grow up to have their Disney fairy-tale dreams come true by getting married in a Disney wedding gown at a Disney resort, which have long been advertised as a haven for honeymooners. The Disney bride can look forward to having her own little princess and starting the cycle all over again.

"But what about the Bratz dolls?" I'm asked during a presentation to parents. "At least they're clearly ethnically diverse. Aren't they better?" The Bratz dolls, "The Girls with a Passion for Fashion," were introduced in 2001 and are now a huge hit all over the world.[12] Chloe, Sasha, Jade, and Yasmin, the Bratz pack, are certainly a more ethnically diverse quartet than Belle, Cinderella, Ariel, and Aurora.

The problem with extolling the Bratz brand for its cultural diversity is that the lessons children learn from toys are not compartmentalized. When children play with a multiracial collection of dolls or action figures with bodies that appear to be anorexic or enhanced by steroids, they can't be expected to get one cultural message and ignore the other. As with the Disney Princesses, the Bratz brand, replete with videos, films, cars, accessories, clothing, and so on, also locks girls into preset scripts rife with stereotypes about women and materialistic values. In addition to their anorexic bodies, they feature heavily made-up faces, and an in-your-face sexuality that's a slightly watered-down version of the pervasive trappings of what's called "raunch culture," often described as pornography gone mainstream.[13]

The Bratz brand doesn't promote dreams of acquiring the accoutrements of royalty. Instead, it promotes dreams of acquiring the trappings of rich teenage sluts. There's the Bratz Forever Diamondz Convertible and even a Bratz limousine—complete with a bar.[14] In the United Kingdom, the Bratz remote-control car is sold with the following pitch: "Hit the streets in style with the Bratz Itsy Bitzy Remote Control Vehicle. Remember, it's not how well you drive, but how good you look while you're doing it."[15] The Bratz are all about conspicuous consumption. While they don't reside in fabulous castles in make believe lands, they have more in common with the Disney Princesses than not. Both brands are competing with Barbie for the hearts, minds, and playtime of little girls.

If we want children to embrace diversity as a value, then providing them with multicultural toys, books, and media that counter prevailing stereotypes is essential. Diversity in toys and media doesn't replace the value of enabling children to live and play in ethnically diverse environments, but it's important for two reasons. One is that minority populations of children have a right to see themselves in the stories that permeate popular culture—inclusion in popular culture is a powerful form of societal validation. The other is that all children benefit from experiencing the similarities and differences among cultures.

At this point, the Disney Princesses are hardly ethnically diverse. While Disney has rolled Mulan, an Asian character, and Pocahontas, a Native American, into the Princess brand, they take a backseat to the white princesses—mainly Belle, Cinderella, and Ariel; Jasmine, the Arabian princess from *Aladdin,* is also included, but when Disney released the movie, there was an outcry from Arabs and Arab Americans that both the hero and the heroine were lighter-skinned, with more Caucasian-looking features, than the other characters, while the villains were drawn with stereotypically Semitic features.[16]

Unless you're the target population, it's hard to understand the depth of anger and pain brought on by living in societies whose cultural and commercial icons perpetuate racism either directly by perpetuating stereotypes or indirectly by exclusion. Although the presence of stereotypes in literature, music, and art is particularly hurtful to the people reduced to caricature, stereotypic fantasy characters are problematic for everyone because they limit our understanding of the complexities of being human and can even incite us to do harm. The notion that we are how we look feeds racism and prejudice. In the extreme, linking physical characteristics to character traits can be dangerous enough to result in genocide. Unless a conscious effort is made to counter them, societal stereotypes may be absorbed by children as young as two.[17]

In 2009, Disney will add a black princess to the brand, but it remains to be seen how integral to the princess line she will be.[18] The African American parents I've talked to see this as a mixed blessing. On the one hand, a black Disney Princess eliminates the terrible pain experienced by black girls who get the message every day that being a princess is desirable and that only white girls can be princesses. On the other hand, for parents who have chosen to opt out of Disney Princess culture, partly because there is no black princess, opting in means allowing their daughters to immerse themselves in a commercial culture that places disproportionate importance on being rich and beautiful and finding a prince to marry. When I asked Enola Aird, a colleague and noted advocate for mothers and children, about the new doll, she urged black parents to be cautious: "We have to ask what values a 'black' princess will teach our children. Will she reinforce white standards of beauty? To what extent will she contribute to what is already an intense overcommercialization of our children's lives? Any benefits will probably be outweighed by the costs."

I have colleagues who have worked for years to push the media industry to make diversity a priority. While there have been some successes, it's an uphill battle. Think about the race and ethnicity of the heroes and villains in popular media and television programs today. How are Arabs portrayed? How many Asian characters are present? Who is considered to be beautiful? Who are the villains? How are African Americans and Latinos characterized?

Psychologist Kenyon Chan, chancellor of the University of Washington Bothell, remembers being brought in to consult on a popular animated cartoon series from the 1980s that was set in medieval Europe and featured the Smurfs—diminutive creatures with large noses and blue skin tones. "I suggested that to make the setting more multicultural, they should integrate the walled city where the action takes place—that they could include people of color in the population, like a sage from Asia or a traveler from Africa," he said. "The writers objected, explaining patiently that people of color didn't really live in medieval Europe." "That's true," Dr. Chan responded. "But neither did the Smurfs!"

Aside from the fact that it's fun, one of the benefits of playing with children is that we can use our shared make believe as an opportunity to introduce new ideas, including those that counter prevailing stereotypes. Mostly I try to follow children's lead whenever I play with them. But there are times—whether I'm playing with children for therapy or just for fun—when I do try to interject alternative points of view.

I once worked with a five-year-old boy who fell in love with my puppet Audrey Duck. He pretended that they got married and had a baby. "When the baby is born you have to say, 'Oh what a beautiful baby,'" he told me. "I'm the father!" he added proudly. Later he invited Audrey and the baby to come watch him play basketball. "You have to cheer for me," he said. After several minutes of sitting on the sidelines, I couldn't resist making Audrey wonder when it would be her turn to play. "This doesn't seem fair," she said to him. "Can't you watch the baby while I play basketball?" At first he resisted, but Audrey kept pointing out the inequity. "Can't we take turns?" she asked. Finally he agreed and tenderly, if reluctantly, relinquished the basketball for the baby—at least for a short time.

One of the problems with children being immersed in brands that span media and toys is that when left to their own devices—which, ideally, is how children should be playing much of the time—the content of their play is dictated by the brands. Immersion in commercial culture, reinforced by multiple viewings and branded toys, means that children's own devices are no longer really theirs. Just as the Spiderman or Power Ranger brands lock little boys into violent play, little girls immersed in the Disney brand can be locked into playing at being helpless females waiting to be rescued.

The same grandmother who put on her bedroom slippers and danced to her demise also uses requests from her Disney-enamored granddaughter to tell princess stories as an opportunity to provide alternative views of gender roles. "I invented a prince who visits the princess and washes the dishes," she says.

In another episode of playing princess, four-year-old Abigail was in the process of simultaneously sorting through princess movies and the story of Passover, the Jewish holiday celebrating the exodus from Egypt. "Let's pretend that I'm a princess drowning in the Red Sea," she said. "And you're the prince coming to rescue me." Plopping herself on the ground she began calling out, "Help me! Help me! I'm drowning!" I stood on the edge of the Red Sea debating my next move. Abigail stopped drowning for a moment to remind me that I was the prince. "Come on!" she said urgently. "Oh dear," I said. "The princess is drowning and I don't even know how to swim. I guess I'll have to try to rescue her." Curious to see what Abigail would do with her helpless princess persona when rescue was not forthcoming, I leaped into the Red Sea, calling out, "Help! Help!" a few times. Suddenly the story changed. "I remember how to swim!" she announced, and promptly came to the rescue, saving herself and the prince.

If our contributions to children's play deviate too far off course or if particular plot points or themes are important to children, they have no hesitation about digging in their heels. When Abigail pretended to be a princess walking through a field of beautiful birds, she closed her eyes and began to wish aloud that her fairy godmother would send her a beautiful bird as a pet. She opened one eye and explained, "You're my fairy godmother." I thought for a minute. "I hear the princess wishing for a bird." I said. "But these are wild birds and they don't like to be pets. I don't think I can send her a bird." Abigail opened both her eyes disapprovingly. "No! No! No!" she said severely. "These are the kind of birds that *like* to be pets." "Oh," I said meekly. And—as Abigail's designated fairy godmother in her very own creation—I sent her one of the imaginary birds in fulfillment of her wishes.

We can do our best to challenge the stereotyped gender roles, unrealistic body types, and materialistic values promoted by brands like the Disney Princesses, Bratz, and Barbie, but even aside from the negative effects I've described, their domination of the toy market for preschool girls is troubling. They contribute to what is primarily a commercially constructed phenomenon that is depriving children of middle childhood, which for the purposes of this book I'll define as between the ages of five or six to ten or eleven.

"Kids are getting older younger," is a common plaint in the toy, clothing, and marketing industries and is used as an excuse to market to seven-year-olds everything from cell phones to thong underpants. The market has usurped the years between six and twelve and transformed them into "tweens," a monolithic consumer demographic of teenage wannabes. Now these industries are working at usurping the preschool years as well. Four- to six-year-olds are referred to as "pre-tweens," and companies like Bonne Bell are targeting little girls with what might be called "pre-makeup," in the form of lip gloss spiked with M&Ms, Dr. Pepper, and other flavors.[19]

Sanitized versions of social-networking sites, which combine elements from sites like MySpace and online fantasy games like Myst, are targeting children as young as five. Some appear to be promoting creativity and individuality, because players get to decorate rooms or clothe an avatar—a symbolic representation of a persona assumed in cyberspace. But in the sites that I've looked at, such as Webkins.com, which is quite popular today, the choices are confined to choosing among pre-designed objects. The pets are cute, the games are fun, and I understand the site's appeal, but there's no escaping the underlying goal, which is to acquire virtual cash to make purchases. These sites, like BarbieGirls.com or Stardoll.com, don't really encourage creativity. Indeed, many seem to be designed primarily to train girls to shop for furniture, clothing, and accessories. Engaging with these sites isn't like actually making doll clothes of your own design from scraps of material or sketching them on paper.[20] When Mattel launched Barbiegirls.com, a toy trends expert commented that girls can "go on the site and chat with their friends, compare outfits, rooms. It's right on target with what girls are looking for."[21]

But are kids actually getting older younger? Girls are reaching puberty earlier than in previous generations. There is, however, no evidence that their cognitive, social, and emotional development, or their judgment, is keeping pace. The frontal cortex—the area of the brain where judgment sits—doesn't develop fully until we reach our midtwenties. Immersion in twenty-first-century commercial culture encourages children to leap directly from preschool to the preoccupations of adolescence—sexuality, identity, and affiliation—before they can possibly understand what any of them mean.

In 2007, a report from the American Psychological Association on the sexualization of young girls stated, "Toy manufacturers produce dolls wearing black leather miniskirts, feather boas, and thigh-high boots and market them to 8- to 12-year-old girls. Clothing stores sell thongs sized for 7- to 10-year-old girls (some printed with slogans such as 'eye candy' or 'wink'; other thongs sized for women and late-adolescent girls are imprinted with characters from Dr. Seuss and the Muppets). In the world of child beauty pageants, 5-year-old girls wear fake teeth, hair extensions, and makeup and are encouraged to 'flirt' onstage by batting their long, false eyelashes. On prime-time television, girls can watch fashion shows in which models made to resemble little girls wear sexy lingerie (e.g., the CBS broadcast of *Victoria's Secret Fashion Show* on December 6, 2005)."[22]

Children are gaining the trappings of maturity at a very young age—language, clothing, and accoutrements. Toy industry executives lament that children stop playing with toys by the age of six, moving on to "grown-up" products such as cell phones, video games, and computers.[23] That they are growing up with technology means that they may grasp the how-to component of computers, MP3 players, cell phones, and handheld electronic games. But where's the evidence that they can cope successfully with the content they encounter or that they don't need what they're missing from spending so much time in front of screens? Even as we marvel at children's technological acumen, we should be wondering: Do six-year-old children who know better than we do how to use a joy stick, surf the Web, master a remote control, also know how to make sense of and protect themselves against the ubiquitous commercialism and its attendant cynicism, sexism, and violence—to say nothing of the pornography—they encounter in virtual reality?

According to the Centers for Disease Control, in 2005 over one-third of American ninth-graders (boys and girls) had already had sex.[24] But the fact that many children are sexually active at fourteen doesn't mean that they are achieving emotional intimacy with their partners or handling relationships particularly well. If children were really getting older younger—if they were actually going through all of the processes of physical, cognitive, social, and emotional maturation more rapidly—then perhaps there would be little cost to them. But that doesn't seem to be the case. Psychologist David Elkind has been writing since the early 1980s about the price paid by hurrying children to grow up too fast—world-weariness, cynicism, and a lack of wonder.[25] At the same time, cultural critic Neil Postman was writing not just about the disappearance of childhood, but about the infantilization of adults.[26] Children seem to be taking longer to achieve real independence than in previous generations. About 40 percent of college graduates are now moving back home after graduation.[27] They aren't moving home, as would be the case in some cultures, to support their families.

They seem to be moving home to save money and to postpone having to take care of themselves.[28]

One of the workshops offered at the 2007 Kid Power marketing conference—the largest such gathering in the United States—was called, "Can KGOY and KSYL Co-exist?" For those out of the loop, the former acronym stands for "Kids are getting older younger." The latter? "Kids are *staying* younger longer."[29]

This does not tell us that children are maturing more rapidly. It implies that something is impeding their attaining adulthood. I think that one of the impediments is that we are depriving them of a chance to experience middle childhood. Perhaps thirty is now the new twenty in part because twelve is also the new twenty—and six is the new twelve. Or, to use marketing jargon, KSYL is the direct consequence of KGOY. Children are missing out on years of being able to use creative play to gain a sense of competence, explore independence, experience constructive problem solving, and learn tools for making meaning.

Unlike the first six years of life, when enormous leaps in learning take place so quickly that children are constantly having to adjust to the precariousness of newly acquired skills, or adolescence, where body changes and issues of identity create a new self-consciousness and surging hormones affect wide swings in emotions, middle childhood is a relatively stable time when skills can be honed, imaginations can run rampant, our bodies don't seem to be out of control, and we can experience a sense of competence about interacting in the world. Children are likely to have at least rudimentary capabilities in reading and math. Their basic physical coordination has come together enough that they can run, jump, hop, and skip. They are honing their cognitive and physical capabilities: reading harder books, attempting more complicated math problems, and learning to play various sports or dance or do gymnastics.

At this point, children's judgment is evolved enough for at least some independent playtime. They are capable of cooperating and can delay gratification enough that they can execute complicated projects both alone and with friends. Adults may be in the house, but they don't have to be in the same room. If there's a safe space to play outside, they are allowed out on their own. At the beginning of middle childhood, adults need to be in the house, but not in the same room. Toward the end, children may be allowed to stay home by themselves for a while.

Middle childhood is a time when children's important influences are moving from home to peers. It can be an incredibly fertile time for intellectual and creative exploration. Although girls are reaching puberty earlier than they used to, it's still a time that is relatively stable physically—at least for some portion of this time kids aren't grappling with great hormonal surges and unwieldy body changes. It's a time when children don't have to worry about their bodies and are able to form friendships with members of the opposite sex without having to worry about sexual overtones.

One of the hallmarks of developmental psychology is the idea of scaffolding—that we evolve cognitively, emotionally, and socially by building on the skills and knowledge we acquire along the way. The developmental psychologist Erik Erikson identified stages of growth and development that revolve around focusing on negotiating specific social and emotional tasks. According to Erikson, we evolve from infancy to adolescence by acquiring a basic sense of trust in the world; building on that trust to establish our autonomy, using our newfound sense of ourselves to experiment with our own creativity; building on our creativity to establish a sense of competence by learning how to tackle and complete complex tasks; and building on our competence to establish our own identities and affiliations.

Another way to think about this is that unless we establish trust as infants, we can't establish autonomy. If we have no sense of self we can't play creatively as preschoolers. If we can't initiate creativity we can't learn to be competent in executing our more complex ideas in middle childhood. If we have never established a sense of ourselves as competent, we will not be able to establish a sense of identity in adolescence as separate from those who care for us.

When it comes to play, what I find most helpful about Erikson's work is that it provides a framework for understanding the content from the point of view of a child's experience and needs. In the introduction to this book I talk about peek-a-boo games as a way of helping babies establish a sense that things or people don't just disappear when we can't see them. Another way to think about them is as one of many ways that babies establish a sense of trust that the world is safe and stable enough for them to begin to practice being independent.

An important component of gaining more independence and autonomy is developing a sense of control over your body. Given that children tend naturally to focus the themes of their creative play around issues of importance to them, it's not surprising that, for toddlers, bathroom play becomes endlessly enjoyable. Ava, age twenty-eight months and just starting to be interested in using a potty, asked her father to take down a paper dragon that had been hanging on a wall. "She wadded up some paper and made it come out of the dragon," he said. "Then she pretended to wipe its bottom. She asked me to help her make diapers for the dragon. We're constantly diapering something or placing one stuffed animal or another on the potty."

Toddlers like Ava are at the early stages of being able to engage in creative play. Over the next few years, depending on her interests and opportunities, she may tell her own stories, make up songs, invent imaginary friends, build block constructions, paint pictures, or sculpt with clay. If her creative explorations are allowed to flourish, she will experience countless hours of pleasure as well as the exhilarating sense of power that comes from generating her own unique creations.

After dessert at a multigenerational family gathering recently, Marley, our resident four-year-old, asked to be excused from the table while the adults remained talking over coffee. She returned a few minutes later draped in a pink, diaphanous ball gown and began to dance around the table making up a song. She started out singing softly, but as she floated and became more immersed in the process, her voice became stronger, increasing in passion and volume. Building to a final, glorious crescendo, she began belting out the song's dramatic conclusion. Flinging out her hands, she sang passionately: "I . . . AM . . . GOD!" She held that last note for several beats. Finally, taking a deep breath, she concluded in rapid staccato. "I MAKE UP ALL THE WORDS!"

If preschoolers are allowed to keep generating play as they grow, its form and content will become more and more complex. Dramatic play may be transformed into actual plays, drawings and paintings become more elaborate, construction projects can become feats of complex engineering. A colleague tells a story about his sons at this age. "They found a huge dead fish on the beach," he remembers. "They wanted to bring it up to show the adults, but they didn't want to have to touch it. Instead, they spent hours weaving this elaborate carrier made of reeds and seaweed that they found on the shore and carried it home, triumphantly." He thought for a moment. "It was like they were playing at being hunter-gatherers."

Think back to your own childhood and your favorite memories of playing. How old were you when you remember your happiest, most engrossing play? Most of the people I ask locate their best memories of playing between the ages of six to about ten. "When you write your book on make believe," a friend in his thirties says, "I hope you include making up our own rules for ball games—in elementary school my friends and I used to play for hours like that." "We used to pretend we were orphans," another friend remembers. "We had all sorts of adventures." "We played with dollhouses," says another, "and made forts, lots of forts."

When children are encouraged to act like teenagers just a few years after shedding their diapers, they miss out on the pleasures of middle childhood. And they are losing years of creative play. According to one study, American nine- to twelve-year-olds spend only one minute a day in pretend play. In 1997—well after both Elkind and Postman began writing about a diminishing childhood—they were spending fifteen minutes. The amount of time six- to eight-year-olds spend in creative play decreased from twenty-five minutes to sixteen minutes during the same time period.[30]

Developmental psychologists believe that children develop at their own rates, but that there's no real shortcut through developmental stages. The road to losing out on middle childhood begins in infancy. It starts by training babies to depend on screens for entertainment and the things they sell for amusement and comfort. Before they can even ask for it, we decorate their cribs, clothing, toys, and diapers with media characters and place them in front of screens at every opportunity. They learn to take their pleasures from the things electronic media provide. By the time children hit preschool, the characters they loved as babies are associated with baby things. "That's baby-ish!" we're apt to hear, about toys, games, and programs that they loved only a few months ago. If children are trained from infancy to take their primary delight from media-generated products, they are likely to seek out other, more seemingly so-phisticated brands. By the time they are entering "tweendom," children are receiving strong commercial messages to stop playing with toys altogether and start getting wired.

It's in their children's infancy and early childhood that par-ents have the best shot of at least postponing or delaying chil-dren's immersion in a stultifying commercial culture. Babies don't nag to be propped in front of screens. The longer parents delay, the longer babies have a chance to develop the capacity to make things happen, to solve problems, to create their own amusements—to generate creative play. But there are powerful forces urging us to turn our babies and toddlers on to screens.

11

Playing for Life

What We All Gain from Make Believe

When Cassidy, at two and a half, finally figured out how to remove every scrap of her clothing, she burst into the living room totally naked. Standing before her bemused parents, she flung her arms out in triumph and proclaimed rapturously, "I escaped my clothes!"

After laughing about this story with Cassidy's father, I found myself acutely aware of the confines of my own clothing in ways that rarely occur to me—the binding bite of elastic, the pull of fabric across my knees, the pinch of leather on weary feet. I was suddenly flooded with precious memories of nakedness, remembering late fall at a mountainside pond in Vermont or lying in bed as a spring breeze blows through an open window. Suddenly I, too, longed to escape my clothes.

I don't buy the romantic vision of childhood as a trouble-free idyll. My own certainly wasn't that way, and I've spent too much time helping children struggle with the gamut of dark, painful feelings rooted in fear and rage. I get nervous when I hear people wax nostalgic about "childhood innocence" because it's often evoked in the context of denying that children have deep feelings, denying them information about sexuality, or lying to them about difficult issues.

For children growing up in reasonably protected environments, innocence is a combination of immature cognition and lack of experience. Our glimpses of it can often be quite poignant. When my granddaughter was three—as the war in Iraq showed no signs of abating—we took her to Canobie Lake Park, a wonderful family-owned amusement park about an hour from home. As we wended our way through the maze of rides for children under forty-eight inches we happened upon one consisting of miniaturized fighter planes each complete with its own stylized machine gun. She didn't ask about the guns and I didn't point them out, but once she was ensconced in the tiny plane, I was curious about what she would do with her weapon. While the other children were merrily shooting away, Marley spent the ride with her face close up to its base peering down at it. Afterward, when asked what she was doing on the ride, she explained, "I was taking pictures." She thought the gun was a camera.

It's hard not to sigh longingly over a child's ignorance of guns, fighter planes, or wholesale slaughter. At three, Marley was lucky—violence and the world at war had not yet impinged on her consciousness. Unlike Iraqi children, or any children living in any war zone or certain pockets of extreme urban poverty, she had no direct experience of it. She seems to have had no experience of media violence, either. Sooner or later—and I expect it will be sooner—the guns will no longer be cameras.

How much we protect children from global injustice, pain, and suffering depends a lot on luck and our own values. But no matter what we do, it is inevitable that as children mature they lose their innocence. It is not inevitable, however, that they become cynical, jaded, dead to the wonders of the world, or overwhelmed with helplessness in the face of great challenge. In a two-year-old's triumphant exodus from garment-induced bondage lies not just the best of childhood, but some of the best qualities of being human—the capacity for wonder, mastery, possibility, and joy—which are, along with other qualities such as love and compassion, central to both spiritual and psychological health.

That young children abound with wonder is one reason to delight in their company. They view with fresh eyes that which we take for granted. Take undressing, for instance, which, except as a prelude to making love, is certainly among the most mundane of experiences: an activity necessary for transition to something else—showering, going to sleep, dressing for work or play. Yet, for Cassidy, being able to remove her clothes is a source of wonder and therefore thrilling. She's amazed at her competence and revels in her newly won freedom. Up to now, until she learned how to rip apart Velcro and snaps, or maybe even unzip or unbutton, she literally *was* trapped in her clothes. Soon she will delight in mastering the even more complex task of putting them on, and she will seek dominion over what she wears. "I dressed all by myself," a four-year-old announces with great pride, "even the buttons!"

It's not a given that we leave wonder behind as we outgrow childhood. In fact, it's an essential component of creativity. The story of Isaac Newton getting bopped on the head with an apple and coming up with gravity seems to be apocryphal, but it's a good metaphor for the necessity of wonder in scientific discovery. Up to that point, we were all tooling along in life, taking the fact that objects fall for granted. Discovering new ways of understanding the world involves a first step of recognizing the extraordinary in what others see as ordinary, or don't see at all. Albert Einstein's sense of wonder, for instance, that a compass always points north led him, as an adult, to explore invisible forces such as magnetic fields.[1] Art, also, depends on wonder. One quality that differentiates great visual artists from excellent draftsmen is their unique way of seeing—the quality of light illuminating a leaf, the pattern left by waves on sand, the particular droop of skin on an aging face—whatever they notice about the world that the rest of us pass over.

Wonder is essential to spirituality. Abraham Joshua Heschel, a great twentieth-century rabbi, activist, and philosopher, invented the term "radical amazement," which begins with a sense of awe that the world around us exists and that we are a part of it—to wonder at the miracle of our own breathing; at volition; at the majesty of the natural world, and our place in it, including the recognition of that which we can and cannot control.[2] But Heschel also asks us to wonder at our capacity for wonder. It's not only amazing that the dogwood trees outside my window blossom year after year, or that a whole, complex sunflower vine can sprout from a single seed. It's also amazing that I am alive and able to experience that amazement. In those moments—amid the strain and distractions of daily life—when we are able to grasp the wonder of our wonder, we live life with heightened consciousness.

If, as Cassidy matures, she is allowed to continue her playful exploration of the world—including the depth, breadth, and limits of her competence to affect her environment and the freedom to recount her experience to willing ears—eventually she will be able to reflect on her experiences and they will have even more meaning for her. There's little room for radical amazement—or even just plain old ordinary amazement—in a life dominated by the insistent distractions of flickering screens, ring tones, beeps, buzzers, and endless information to process. In addition to a large dose of humility, we need the time and space to savor experience for its own sake. We need to be able to play.

There's also a link between sustaining capacities for play and playfulness into adulthood and realizing our unique potential for living a satisfying life—for seeking out experiences congruent with who we really are and through which we find meaning and purpose in living. Play is our first experience with the enjoyment and challenge of intrinsic motivation—of choosing to engage in an activity for its inherent value, not because it brings us some external reward or satisfies a biological drive. Volition is a central component of achieving what psychologist Mihaly Csikszentmihalyi calls "optimal experience" or "flow," which he describes as feeling competent, in sync with the world, and utterly alive.[3] In describing flow, Csikszentmihalyi makes an important distinction between pleasure and enjoyment. Pleasure is the feeling of contentment and sense of equilibrium we get when our sensory needs are met. Pleasure can be restorative, but it does not lead to growth or change. Unlike pleasure, enjoyment and optimal experience are achieved with effort—when we successfully take on challenges, for instance, master new skills, or explore new ideas. Optimal experience embodies enjoyment but not necessarily pleasure.

For children, flow is embodied in the exultation they exude in play. For adults, the tasks that lead to optimal experience may not exactly be play, but, in addition to volition, the way we approach those tasks shares many qualities of playfulness; savoring an activity for itself, intense concentration, and a certain precariousness manifest in difficult but ultimately conquerable challenges that lead to a sense of mastery.

Csikszentmihalyi's work has led him to people who can turn even a repetitive, seemingly boring activity into optimal experience. He describes a factory worker in a very dirty, boring job who found ways to challenge himself by setting goals for speed or pushing himself to understand the workings of all of the machinery in the shop. In a sense, he was "playing" with his job, and it was his capacity to play, not the external circumstance of his work, that made it enjoyable.[4]

When it comes to living a meaningful life, the form our creativity takes is not important. Rather, what's important is that we are able to gain access to it, that we recognize its existence and nurture its expression. It is in play that we are free to be creative and, as I am reminded repeatedly in my therapeutic work with children, make believe is a powerful tool for getting in touch with who we really are. That brings me back to Cassidy one more time. When I shared her story with Tim Kasser, a psychologist at Knox College, whose work on intrinsic motivation, materialism, and meaning has informed my thinking on play, he responded immediately to the metaphoric aspect of her delight. Clothing can be seen to represent the demands of society and the constrictions that socializing places upon us. Her drive to rid herself of clothing reminds us of chaffing against societal demands and our desire to be free of the conventions of society. Cassidy's world has expanded and her understanding of what being dressed means has altered forever. Now that she has the possibility of removing them at will, her clothes and why she's wearing them will take on whole new meanings.

With her parents' help, Cassidy will wrestle with the complexities of living in a society that dictates, at least through its mores, when and where she can remove her clothes. In the process she will begin to learn the meaning of social conventions and that having gained the ability to do something—like flinging off our clothes—doesn't necessarily mean that we can do it any time we please. As she encounters these restrictions from the external world, she can play about them in an imaginary world over which she has dominion. One of the games Cassidy enjoyed around this time involved lots of ordering her parents around when they played together. As the demands of socialization impinge on her freedom, as she subjugates some of her desires to social convention, she will still, if she's allowed to continue to play, have opportunities to nurture, preserve, and protect her true, spontaneous, creative self.

I'm not against socialization per se. I get concerned when the forces of socialization become too dominant, and especially when they emanate from antisocial motivations like greed or the consolidation of power. Since we live in an interdependent society, however, we need to take other people into account. If we care about other people, and if we believe, as I do, that life brings an inherent debt to the rest of the world, then we have an obligation to balance our own needs and desires with what's best for society. At the same time, we need to be able to sort through hype and recognize the difference between wisdom and a sales pitch. In order to do any of this, we have to develop, first of all, a sense of self in relation to others. We have to know who we are and what we value.

I was speaking at a conference recently where each presenter was asked to identify the greatest threat to childhood today. It's not surprising that climate change was the one that came up most often. I, however, took a step back and chose greed. If, to fill corporate coffers, we immerse children in a commercial culture designed to train them from birth to value consumption above all else, we are likely to raise an insatiable population of consumers blind to anything but the fulfillment of their immediate needs. Greed is a significant component of global warming. After the conference, since I was immersed in writing this book, I began to think about the links between the commercialization of children's play and global warming. I started thinking about excess packaging and how plastics are made, about how a component of toy marketing is convincing children that one just isn't enough and that the purpose of dolls like Barbie or the Bratz is to sell their accessories. Enabling creative play gives children a shot at building more inner resources and being less dependent on external sources for pleasure and enjoyment. If we encourage children to hone their own imagination and inventiveness, they are less apt to need the transient novelty of a new toy to generate excitement or hold their interest. By letting children develop their inborn capacity for creative play, we are helping them develop skills and values that lend themselves to better stewardship of the earth and its natural resources.

In contrast, by preventing children from playing, we are depriving them of chances to get to know themselves in relation to the rest of the world. One problem with raising children in the midst of cultural values dominated by unfettered capitalism and promulgated by ever-present electronic media is that it becomes increasingly difficult to withstand the seductive insistence of commercially constructed expectations and demands. If we don't know who we are—if we can't hang on to a sense of ourselves in the distractions of blinding glitter, deafening noise, and psychologically sophisticated come-ons—then we are less likely to know the difference between what we want and what we are told we want. We are less likely to question and unlikely to resist societal coercion, even if it is ultimately harmful to ourselves or other people. We may be good consumers but lousy citizens.

The links between nurturing democracy and nurturing play—and the threat that a market-dominated society poses to both—became piercingly clear to me when, in 2007, President George W. Bush lauded Julie Aigner-Clark, the creator of Baby

Einstein, in his State of the Union address. After I picked myself up off the floor, I realized how fitting it was for that particular president to single out Aigner-Clark as a stellar example of entrepreneurship. The Baby Einstein Company (which she sold to Disney for more than $20 million in 2001) and the Bush administration actually had a great deal in common. Both have specialized in brilliantly crafted, hugely successful, false, and deceptive marketing to promote their brands. The most horrifying example of the Bush administration's deceptive marketing and manipulation of fear was the war in Iraq—sold to us through unsubstantiated claims of weapons of mass destruction and by hyping a link that didn't exist between Saddam Hussein and Osama bin Laden. As noted in Chapter 3, Disney has marketed Baby Einstein through unsubstantiated claims that its videos are educational for babies by hyping a link that doesn't exist between its brand and learning. Both exploit fear as a tool for marketing. Both have relied on building a passive and accepting media audience.

In making this comparison, I do not mean to trivialize the damage done by the war in Iraq or the ongoing tragedy of the carnage there. Certainly no infant has died watching Baby Einstein. At best, baby videos look like fun; at worst, they appear to be merely inane. But the fact is, media companies like Disney, which deceptively market screen time as beneficial to babies, are doing actual harm. Particularly relevant to the future state of our democratic union is research suggesting that the more time babies spend in front of a TV, the less time they spend in creative play.[5] The skills children learn in play—critical thinking, initiative, curiosity, problem solving, and creativity as well as the more ephemeral qualities of self-reflection and empathy—are essential to thriving in and protecting a democratic society. These are in contrast to the values children learn from a commercially dominated media: unthinking brand loyalty, impulse buying, the notion that self-worth is defined by ownership, and a belief that consumption is the solution to all ills. Let's not forget that, after the World Trade Center was attacked, we were told by our government to go shopping.

One potential consequence of the baby-media industry's success in scamming American parents is that screen-saturated, play-deprived babies will grow into screen-dependent adults, without the will or capacity to question what they're being sold. During the buildup to the Iraq War, Andrew Card, the Bush administration's chief of staff, was asked why the administration waited until September to promote the invasion. He replied, "From a marketing point of view, you don't introduce new products in August."[6] Do we want to raise a generation of die-hard consumers trained from birth to buy into war as just another product, or do we want to raise democratic citizens? If it's the latter, then one thing we need to do is find ways to support children's right to play.

Once we expand our notion of playing beyond discrete activities to thinking about play as an essential tool for living—for finding meaning, experiencing who we really are, and understanding the power and limits of our place in the world—the choice to nurture make believe becomes a moral, ethical, and sociopolitical stance. It's strange to think of make believe as countercultural, but at this time, in this particular society, it is. The dominant culture so strongly dictates against creative play that we have to take active steps—at home, in our communities, and at a policy level—to ensure its presence in children's lives.

Sasha, Your Peas Are Calling You

Nurturing Play in a Culture Bent on Squelching It

When my daughter was almost two she entered that wonderful/terrible stage of development characterized by the word "No." She said it a lot—even to things she actually wanted to do. It was a pleasure to watch her burgeoning sense of self and I rejoiced in her determination and strength of character. But at the same time, she was sometimes hard to live with. One day, when I was complaining about our daily power struggles to my friend Zoe, whose daughter was a year older, she said casually, "You know, Susan, I find that puppets are really useful." "Oh!" I exclaimed excitedly. "Puppets! What a great idea! I never thought of that!" A peculiar expression came over her face. "Susan," she replied with that tone tinged with amused exasperation we tolerate only from our closest friends, "I learned it from you."

Remembering to play with our children, and hanging on to our own playfulness in the throes of raising them, can be difficult. Avoiding unnecessary conflict is only one of myriad reasons to play with children. The sheer joy is reason enough. Never mind that play facilitates learning, promotes problem solving, engenders empathy, builds social skills, and lays the foundation for leading a rich and meaningful life. After my enlightening talk with Zoe, phrases like "Sasha, your peas are calling you!" became a standard means of helping her tear herself away from whatever she was immersed in at the moment dinner was ready. Her socks argued about which would have the honor of going on first, as did the sleeves of her shirts. Make believe is no magic bullet, but life with a two-year-old grappling with autonomy got just a little bit easier and a whole lot more fun.

As hard as it may be for overstressed parents to remember to play with their children, it's never been harder for children to play on their own. Just about everything in our society dictates against it. Make believe flourishes best when a community of caring adults provides children with gifts that can't be bought: time, space, and silence. Some of the biggest hurdles to children's creative play are rends in our social fabric rooted in capitalism run amok. Play erodes when self-interest trumps public interest; when we neglect public parks and playgrounds; when we withdraw support from public schools; when we conflate public health with commercial interests; and when corporate profits take precedent over children's well-being, flooding them with incessant noise from gizmos and gadgets that prevent them from listening to their own unique voices.

Children are deprived of play when schools cut gym, recess, and classes in the arts; when educational policy dictates that they are treated as objects, even in preschool, rather than as active, developing, learners; and when parents who can afford it overschedule them with "enrichment" classes and organized sports. They are prevented from playing when parents short on financial resources and time are left with no choice but to leave kids home alone after school where hours with electronic media seems much safer than letting them venture out in what feels like—and in some instances may be—an unsafe world.

On a national level, we need to work for policies that support families, provide children with meaningful education, preserve open space, and protect children from corporate marketing. Family leave time, flexible work schedules, equal pay, and paid vacations would give some relief to stressed-out parents. So would universal child care. If day-care centers and after-school programs were adequately staffed by adequately paid professionals trained to facilitate creative play, they would provide opportunities for make believe to children who aren't getting it at home.

We need to find ways to ensure children opportunities to engage in nature—for that matter, we need to make sure that there's enough nature left for engagement. Being out in the natural world inspires creativity. J.K. Rowling, author of the Harry Potter series, attributes her imagination to the time she spent growing up rather isolated near the Forest of Dean in Britain.[1] Research backs up her personal observation, suggesting that more creative play takes place in natural green spaces than in traditional playgrounds.[2] Educational policies that nurture children's innate drive for active exploration, rather than treating them as receptacles for facts, would by definition encourage creative play. It's not that I'm against facts. I actually see the value in learning multiplication tables, even with easy access to calculators. But I also believe that school is for helping children learn how to learn, and that play is a central component to active learning.

We need to stop mistaking commerce for community. Corporations are all too happy to leap into the breach when we lose the political will to build a society based on the responsibilities and benefits of publicly supported institutions. That comes at a terrible cost. A play space at McDonald's is not the same as a public park. Ronald McDonald going into schools to promote exercise is not a substitute for gym or recess. Schools report that kids seem to enjoy the latest trend to use Nintendo's Wii game, Dance Dance Revolution, in schools for physical education.[3] But given the chance and adequate support, they would enjoy running around on their own as well—and be free from the debilitating message that screens are essential to living

Speaking of screens, that brings me to what authors Dimitri Christakis and Fred Zimmerman call "the elephant in the living room."[4] The need to encourage play requires discouraging children's dependence on media and commercial culture. As the singer, songwriter, and activist Raffi Cavoukian is fond of saying, we have to "de-screen" children. I would add that we also need to do the best we can to delay getting them "screened" for as long as possible. And even as I write that, I once again hear Audrey's voice.

AUDREY: That's soooo last century.

ME: It's forward thinking.

AUDREY: It's quaint.

ME: It's avant-garde.

AUDREY: It's stodgy.

ME: It's impassioned.

AUDREY (*outraged*): Are we saying that fifteen minutes here and there in front of the tube is going to destroy babyhood?

ME: No. We're saying that the decision about when and how to introduce screen media into a child's life shouldn't be taken lightly—and neither should the decision about how much they watch.

AUDREY: We're not just anti-screen—we're pro-guilt!

The last thing I want to do is make parents feel guilty. That's why I believe we have to work for social change, even if it seems like an overwhelming task. It's hard to be a parent today, and as a society we don't support policies that could make it easier. Meanwhile, ever since the 1980s, when widespread concern about latchkey kids became a gold mine for corporations sponsoring after-school television programming, marketers have been selling us on the notion of screen media as essential for child care.[5] What's worrisome is that they've been so successful that some of the parents I talk to even believe that they are inadequate to the task of raising children without screens. "How can I take a shower? How can we go on car trips? How can I cook dinner?" are common complaints. Ironically, it's like a self-fulfilling prophecy. Once children become dependent on electronic media to stave off boredom or calm down, their families are more likely to become dependent on screens for functioning.

The longer we can put off incorporating screen media into children's daily routine, the more opportunity they have for developing those skills and attributes that will prevent their dependence on it and allow them to play creatively. Given the number of babies engaged with screens on a daily basis, and the percentage of parents who believe that they are beneficial, it's clear that the media and marketing industries are doing a great job convincing parents that screens are essential to child-rearing. That's why we need to hold companies accountable for their advertising claims. Toward that end, in the spring of 2006 the Campaign for a Commercial-Free Childhood filed a complaint to the Federal Trade Commission (FTC) against three baby media companies, Disney's Baby Einstein, Brainy Baby, and BabyFirstTV, for false and deceptive advertising.[6] We believe that media companies claiming that a product is educational should be required to document the veracity of that claim. As I write, our complaint is still under review. I have no idea how the FTC will act, but I do know that since we filed, Baby Einstein has made changes to its Web site, modifying some of the claims we mention in our complaint. We're hoping that the FTC will set policy that precludes marketing these videos as educational unless companies can produce research documenting what babies actually learn from them.[7]

I've written elsewhere about the need to set societal limits on corporate marketing that targets children. We also need to find a way to provide parents, and especially parents-to-be, with honest information—not corporate-sponsored marketing hype—about the pros and cons of screen media, the value of creative play, and how to facilitate make believe even in the context of stressful lives.

AUDREY: Nickelodeon wants me to play.

ME: You mean the TV station?

AUDREY (*smirking*): Uh-huh.

ME: Really?

AUDREY: Yes. And President Clinton and the Heart Association are helping Nick help me play. I go to their Let's Just Play Web site every day, and it has links to all sorts of suggestions for me about playing and staying healthy. I expect that they're very good suggestions, too. (*She pauses*) Nickelodeon cares about me.

ME: You *expect* that they're good suggestions? Don't you know?

AUDREY: Not really. Every time I go to the Web site I get sidetracked. I like to see what's new with my favorite Nick characters—like . . . like SpongeBob and Dora and Jimmy Neutron. And guess what? When I click on their pictures I get to play games about them online. For free! It's way cool. I don't have time to look at the play stuff. (*She switches*

gears) Oh yeah, that reminds me. Next time we go on vacation . . . ?

ME (*braced for something, but I'm not sure what*): Yes?

AUDREY: Can we stay at a Holiday Inn? They have Nickelodeon
Suites! I learned that from Let's Just Play, too.[8]

At best, a corporate-owned Web site that features links to
online games and ads for branded vacations sends confusing
messages about play. At worst, such sites undermine it. When
a media company like Nickelodeon has a huge financial stake
in keeping children glued to a screen, why would it ever actually promote play? Since corporations are legally bound to place
shareholder profits above all else, there's no way that Nickelodeon, or any media company, can wholeheartedly urge children to embrace playing. A nation of children at play would
undermine Nick's profits.

What makes campaigns like Nickelodeon's Let's Just Play
even more confusing is their partnership with public health organizations like the American Heart Association, respected
public figures like Bill Clinton, and advisory boards of educators and health-care professionals who may be well paid for
their endorsements. In Chapters 2 and 3, I described the ways
that corporations seduce parents and children away from play.
The public health and education communities are susceptible
to seduction as well. Cash for consulting, corporate funding for
research, and the promise of widespread publicity for under-
funded nonprofits create dual, and sometimes conflicting, interests for educators and the guardians of public health. There
are bound to be conflicts in accepting money for research or solutions to a societal problem from a company that's profiting
from, as well as causing or sustaining, that problem.

Some of my public health colleagues tell me that there's no point in even trying to set limits on corporate America's grip on play, and that corporate programs like Nickelodeon's Let's Just Play are better than no effort at all. I don't agree. By exploiting the chasm caused by diminished public support for play, programs like Nickelodeon's lull us into believing that there's no difference between public funding and corporate dollars spent to promote a brand. For instance, studies of the tobacco industry's campaigns to stop smoking suggest that these kinds of corporate efforts don't work.[9]

Similar arguments for supporting the corporate co-optation of play—of the "if you can't beat them, join them" variety—come up a lot in the struggle to convince parents to give babies a chance to grow and develop independent of screens. Given the lack of research to show that screen time is beneficial to babies, the small but growing body of research suggesting that it may be harmful, and the American Academy of Pediatrics' recommendation of no screen time for children under two, it should be relatively simple to convince parents to keep the first few years of children's lives screen-free. Babies aren't nagging to watch. Toddlers aren't subject to peer pressure. Parents have more control over their children's activities during the first two years of life than at any other point. Allowing children at least a few screen-free years will give them a chance to develop skills and attributes that lend themselves to creative play and will help them resist becoming adults in thrall to commercial media and the products they sell. It's easier to inculcate good habits than it is break unhealthy ones. Yet 40 percent of three-month-old babies are regular consumers of screen media.[10] Despite widespread evidence that children are spending too much time with screens and not enough time in play, the public health community is anything but united on this issue.

The argument I hear most often from colleagues for not publicly supporting the AAP's recommendation goes like this: "It's not that I think that it's good for children to be heavy consumers of screen media—or even that babies should be watching—but it's clear that parents are committed to using videos with babies; they don't want to hear about its potential harms." Another argument goes: "Media companies and marketers have all the power and money, and parents aren't going to listen to our suggestions. Besides, it's risky. We're likely to get trashed in a corporate-controlled press." Finally, there's this: "If parents are relying on media to raise their babies and toddlers, let's make videos for babies that are at least thoughtful and age-appropriate. It's better for babies to be watching a video made just for them than to be watching, say, *Lost* or reruns of *The Sopranos.*"

While I'm fond of both *Lost* and *The Sopranos* myself, I certainly don't think that either are good viewing fare for children. I agree that today's overworked, overstressed, undersupported parents who consume a lot of electronic media themselves may not want to hear that screen time isn't good for babies. But I also believe that parents deserve honest information, and that the public health community should have enough integrity to take a stand, based on the best available evidence, on what's best for children.

One hurdle to getting the public health community to take strong positions—like the AAP's recommendation on babies and screen medias—that may put a dent in corporate profits is that, in the absence of adequate public funding, corporations fund research on health and education, support other kinds of projects as well, and can bring unprecedented publicity to the missions of struggling nonprofits. It's an effective way of silencing opposition. Shortly after Coca-Cola gave a $1 million grant to the American Academy of Pediatric Dentistry (AAPD), the

AAPD's executive director, Dr. John Rutkauskas, said the relationship between soft drinks and cavities is "not clear."[11] Despite protestations to the contrary, research suggests that taking funding for research from corporations with a vested interest in the results does seem to affect findings.[12] When the lines between corporations and the public health community are blurred, parents lose access to objective sources of information that would help them make informed decisions about conundrums like the role media should play in children's lives.

An example of how that occurred in the baby video controversy is when Sesame Workshop decided to get into the baby media business and convinced Zero to Three, one of the most respected public health advocacy groups for young children, to partner with them on *Sesame Beginnings,* a video series for babies as young as six months.[13] Once they had a vested interest in a baby video series, Zero to Three lost its credibility as an objective source of information for parents on that issue. That Sesame Workshop convinced a well-respected academic researcher to consult on the series and accept funding for researching its effectiveness is equally troubling. There's an inherent conflict of interest in consulting on a project and then conducting its summative research.

We need public funding for public health research on baby media in particular, and on play in general, and we need to support advocacy organizations so that they aren't tempted to form partnerships that may compromise their effectiveness.

Promoting play is going to take a united effort to change what have become ingrained behaviors. We need to invest in educating people about play the way we've invested in changing behaviors around seat belts or tobacco use. Once we view the demise of play as a public health problem, it becomes clear that we need a massive public health campaign, free of corporate partnerships, promoting clear and unambivalent messages about the importance of play and how to make it happen. The campaign needs to target policymakers, educators, health-care professionals, child-care providers, and parents—and especially parents-to-be. We need to promote play and alternatives to screen time not just in pediatricians' offices, hospital clinics, day-care centers, and schools but in obstetricians' offices, birthing classes, preparenting classes, and prenatal clinics as well.

The good news is that there is a burgeoning resurgence of interest in play and a growing sense that it needs to be addressed as a sociopolitical issue. In August 2007, when Mattel and other toy companies issued recalls of toys containing lead, the *New York Times* printed an editorial suggesting that one solution for parents was to stop buying their children commercial toys.

> Might it not be possible, for a young child, anyway, to fend off her inevitable molding into a loyal consumerist, and to delay the acquisition of acute brand-recognition skills?
>
> Maybe she doesn't need a talking dump trunk or Barbie with the Malibu beach house. Let her flail on a saucepan with a wooden spoon. Give her paper and crayons. Let her play to her own narrative, not Dora the Explorer's or SpongeBob's.[14]

Advocacy organizations such as the Alliance for Childhood and the American Association for the Child's Right to Play (AACRP) are working to restore play to American childhood. The Alliance is spearheading efforts to incorporate play into classrooms, and the AACRP is working to bring back recess. Both are involved in bringing play back into local communities by working with departments of parks and recreation and in bringing it back into schools. It's encouraging that traditional summer camps based on play and exploring nature are experiencing a resurgence.[15]

I also take heart from the new No Child Left Inside movement, which is working to encourage schools and community groups to ensure children time outside in green spaces. It's based on the premise that unless we intervene, children are going to grow up permanently divorced from nature, which will hinder their social, emotional, and cognitive development.[16]

From the perspective of fostering social change, it's hopeful that environmentalists and proponents of play are beginning to collaborate on creating outdoor spaces that promote creative play—and both should be working to limit corporate marketers' access to children. The goals of these three movements are intertwined. The more children can play creatively, the less dependent they are on consuming toys and gadgets whose production and packaging harms the environment, and the less likely they are to hold acquisition as a primary value. The more shielded children are from corporate marketing, the more likely they are to play creatively. The more children learn to value the environment, the more conscious they will be of the environmental impact of the products that advertising lures them to buy, and the more likely they are to spend time in nature, which facilitates creative play. There are signs that this collaboration and cross-fertilization may be happening. Recently, for the first time, the Campaign for a Commercial-Free Childhood was invited to participate in a national environmental conference and received a second call, for a different conference on the environment, a few days later. In 2006, CCFC partnered with environmental and labor groups to successfully convince TIAA-CREF, the world's largest pension fund, to remove Coca-

Cola from its social-choice account, because the company's policies on marketing to children, on labor, and on the environment are not socially responsible. One of the ways Coca-Cola targets young children is through Coke-branded toys.

"But social change takes time," laments a parent when I speak at a parent-teacher meeting. "What am I supposed to do with my children now? We're not a 'pull the plug, move to the woods' kind of family. I do care about imagination and creativity, but I want to live in a city and send my children to public school—and I don't want to give up commercial culture completely. What should parents like me do?"

Encouraging children to play is probably easiest for parents who are raising their children outside of mainstream culture—those who throw out their televisions or homeschool their children. It also helps if they can afford to send children to private schools that eschew commercialism and promote creative, critical thinking, and if they live in a community that supports their values. Then they don't have to deal with so many countervailing messages. But these options aren't financially feasible, or even appealing, to most people. Much as dropping out sometimes seems attractive to me, that's not how I raised my family and it feels hypocritical to recommend it. Instead, my husband and I chose to set limits and boundaries while living and participating in mainstream culture. Of course, that was easier to do when our children were young than it is today. My stepson is now thirty-six, my daughter is twenty, and the threats to play are significantly worse today than when either of them was little. I live in an urban community known for its progressive values; it was easy for us to find a play-based preschool, and play was not as threatened in public schools as it is today. We could afford summer camps that reinforced our values. It also helped that my husband and I are pretty much united in our social and political beliefs.

But even with all that support, and in a somewhat easier time, we had to make a conscious effort to keep the threats to play at bay. We had, and still have, a television—but only one and we set limits on viewing. As a family policy, we didn't buy toys advertised on television—but we didn't, as some families do, throw them out when they arrived as gifts on birthdays and holidays. In other words, we did the best we could, given who we are.

There are lots of steps that families can take to incorporate creative play into their lives. If we want our children to play, for instance, we can be thoughtful about the toys we choose for them, and—at least when they are young—those we allow them to choose for themselves. Remember that:

- We tend to buy our children way too many toys.
- The toys sold through commercial media and the toys linked to media programs often tend to limit children's creative play rather than encourage it.
- When it comes to picking toys that encourage creative play, less is more. Toys that move and speak on their own have less creative value because they deprive children of opportunities to move and speak for them.
- Toys that can be used in lots of different ways encourage creative play, as do toys that promote open-ended play. A block-building kit that can build only one thing diminishes the creative value of playing with blocks.
- If we think about what babies really want and need, there is no reason to buy them electronic toys or toys based on media characters. They aren't asking for

them. All the world's a toy to a baby. Babies are apt to fall in love with whatever stuffed bear or funny-looking creature becomes familiar to them, regardless of its star status. Besides, generic creatures don't turn up on candy wrappers and sugar cereal boxes—they aren't designed to sell you or your baby other products.

- It's true that taking a shower can be challenging if you're home alone with a toddler, and that makes relying on baby videos appealing. But if you care about play and want to take a shower, make sure that your child is safe, has something engaging within reach—and then take a quick one. Even if toddlers get irritable for the few minutes they're left on their own, it's a good lesson in learning how to generate their own stimulation. Having to amuse or soothe themselves for short periods of time can be a springboard for children's creativity and for developing the ability to enjoy playing alone.

- Cooking dinner is another time when parents resort to screen time for babies and toddlers. Instead, try having a bottom drawer in the kitchen filled with safe kitchen equipment to explore and play with. Changing what's in the drawer every so often creates novelty and will help children sustain interest while you cook. Baby swings, high chairs, and playpens can keep children safe if you need to focus on preparing a meal. Try giving children access to a few toys so they can occupy themselves, or try listening to music, singing, or talking to them as you cook. A little soapy water and a few plastic cups can occupy young children for a really long time.

It we want children to play, we need to set limits on screen media and commercial culture. That gets increasingly hard to do as they grow, especially if they aren't used to limits to begin with. As children get older, choices about toys and play become more complicated. Unless you are really removed from mainstream society, it's likely that the well-financed, often irresistible lure of media and marketing is going to affect them and their play. Once children start elementary school and their primary identification begins to shift away from family, their friends' preferences and standards begin to carry more weight. Parents have significantly less control over children's choice of companions, and kids begin to spend after-school time with friends whose families may have different values than yours. Perhaps they allow more TV, buy more junk food or media-linked toys, or allow more video games and computer time than you do at home.

What happens next depends on you, your values, and your child's temperament, interests, vulnerabilities, and inclinations. Some children are less susceptible to peer influences. Some are more interested in pleasing adults. Some are less assertive about their desires. Some are more acquisitive. What's important to remember is that the more time children spend in front of screens and the more time they spend with commercialized toys when they're little, the less chance they're going to have to play and gain the benefits from playing—and the fewer resources they're going to have for generating play. Unless we cordon off time and space for play, it's just not likely to happen. Screens, not make believe, are the default leisure activities for children today.

We need to work together to create a society that nurtures make believe. In the meantime, every opportunity we provide for children to play is a gift to them. If you're looking for ways to facilitate play within your own family, you may wish to consider some of the following ideas.

- Build unstructured time—free of lessons, organized sports, and screens—into your children's lives that will give them a chance to learn how to generate their own creative play.
- Give your children chances to play on their own. If they are old enough to be responsible and your neighborhood is safe, encourage them to play outdoors and provide opportunities for them to invent their own games away from adult intervention. For children too young to be unsupervised, giant cardboard boxes or a tent made out of a sheet strung across two chairs can give them the delightfully exciting illusion of independence.
- If you allow children regular access to screen media, set limits on time and institute the tradition of some time—even if it's one evening a week—that's screen-free. Use this time to play games, read aloud, be silly, go outside, cook, do craft projects, enjoy nature, or anything else that you all enjoy that facilitates play and creativity.
- Make sure that there really is a balance in your child's life between commercially driven activities and creative play. Be conscious about your choices and remember that while TV programs, computer games, and Web sites can be entertaining, most of them don't promote creative play.
- Recognize the difference between art supplies and prefabricated art projects that limit creativity. When I was a child, my mother abhorred coloring books for

the limitations they imposed on creative expression; this didn't stop me from acquiring them on occasion. I actually have fond memories of coloring books, but they have to do with perfecting a skill (coloring within the lines) and not the rich, joyful experience of transporting myself—with friends or alone—into worlds of my own creation.

- Invest, from infancy, in toys promoting open-ended play. Great suggestions for age-appropriate toys can be found at www.truceteachers.org, the Web site for Teachers Resisting Unhealthy Children's Entertainment (TRUCE). Honor your children's interests and predilections. Some prefer building, mechanics, or art projects to dramatic play. Blocks of any sort help children develop visual and spatial awareness, balance, rudimentary awareness of math concepts, and, on a deeper level, problem-solving skills, including patience, resilience, curiosity, and tenacity. Toy doctor's kits, firefighter's hats, and other accoutrements of dress-up have long been viewed in early childhood education circles as tools for helping children explore the adult world. I often think that one of the most important lessons children can learn comes from the physical experience of fitting together puzzle pieces. If a puzzle piece doesn't work one way, then try it another way. And if it doesn't work at all, try another piece. It's a great metaphor for all sorts of problem solving.

- As you're looking for preschools, or day care, choose play-based programs that don't rely on showing movies and videos to entertain the children.

- If you enjoy films and want to share that experience with your children, but don't want to get caught up in commercial clutter, try renting old movies that you can enjoy together. Speaking of films, make an effort to read children the book on which a movie is based before they see it on the screen. I'm not against books being made into films, but making sure that children are exposed to the print version first gives them a chance to exercise their own visions of favorite characters before Hollywood imposes its vision.

Car trips, train rides, waits in restaurants and doctors' offices can be stressful for families, which is why purveyors of screen media have found a market in portable screens, including those in the backseat of cars. But they can also be opportunities for play if children aren't dependent on screen media to get them from one place to another without being bored or cranky.

In 2005, as the cell phone industry was first marketing the notion of media programs on cell phones as tools to entertain children, a spokesperson for Verizon announced, "Parents who have some time with a kid are finding [video downloads on cell phones] to be a great diversion . . . say, in a dentist's waiting room or in a grocery line."[17] Ken Heyer, a market researcher for ABI Technologies, put it this way in the *New York Times*: "It's really convenient because there's only so much 'I Spy' that you can play . . ."[18]

Time spent waiting can be aggravating, but it is also an opportunity to help children develop internal resources for staving off boredom. The thing about playing I Spy, of which Mr. Heyer spoke so disparagingly, is that any game requiring young children to find and identify objects around them by color, shape, or size helps them get in the habit of being engaged with their surroundings. It's true that we can only play I Spy for so long, but there are other games to help children pass the time while they're between places that keep them interacting with their environment. Once my daughter learned to read, whenever we had time to kill where signs were available, we played a game based on how many words we could find in a word or phrase on a sign in front of us—like "entertainment," "No Smoking," or "antihistamine." When she was young, we played cooperatively. As she got older, it became a competition.

Paper-and-pencil games like Hangman, or the lesser-known Jotto, can be played on napkins in restaurants. If word games aren't your thing, even four-year-olds can participate in drawing games. My family is fond of the one where someone draws a head, folds the piece of paper over, another person draws the upper body and folds that over, the next person draws the lower body, and the last person draws the legs—which can also be played with napkins. Counting games help pass the time as well. One that I learned from my mother, and played with my daughter whenever we walked someplace, involves guessing the number of sidewalk squares between where we stood and some landmark down the block.

It's true that if you provide children with a screen device when you go on car trips, take public transportation, or go for their annual physical, the periods you spend waiting may be more restful and easier to manage. But such convenience comes at a cost. It fosters dependence on screens to get through a day, and prevents children from getting in the habit of noticing, and engaging with, the world around them.

At a time when most children's toys and media preclude creative play, we can actively encourage children to get in the habit of imagining beyond the stories they hear and the pictures they see. Ask questions about content that have no right answer. For instance, I was telling the story of Goldilocks and the three bears to a two-year-old visitor recently, and when I got to the part where Goldilocks finds the bears' house in the woods I asked, "And what color was the house?" There was a moment's silence. Just as her mother began explaining that their storybook of Goldilocks didn't mention the color of the bears' house, the little girl shouted, "Red!" Ask children to participate in the stories you read or tell—to contribute what they visualize, to go beyond the text to add something of their own creation.

Try sharing the activities you enjoy most with your children, especially when they are young. My bias, of course, is the animation of inanimate objects, which can be a continual source of joy and wonder to young children. As my friend Zoe reminded me, talking through puppets, stuffed animals, dolls, or frozen peas is a wonderful way to engage children, and often a great way to help them over the hump of distasteful tasks or expose them to a point of view they may not be eager to share. When parents give voice to a fantasy creature who enthusiastically mirrors their children's reluctance to go to bed, eat dinner, stay with a babysitter, or what have you, they often find their kids respond by taking a parental role. With huge enjoyment, children get to be understanding but firm, rigid, or even mean about making these creatures do exactly what they themselves don't want to do. They are also often enchanted at the thought of being a good example or demonstrating exactly how to execute a particular task they had previously refused to complete.

By the time my daughter entered first grade, she was less entranced when I made her socks argue, but she was at a different point in her cognitive, social, and emotional development. Her capacity for reason had developed enough that she was more able to anticipate the consequences of not getting dressed or not eating dinner than when she was younger. Besides, asserting her independence wasn't a primary motivation the way it was at two or would be in a few more years.

Remember that make believe provides wonderful opportunities for children to rehearse life challenges. Doctor's appointments, routine injections, or first days of school are all fodder for parent-child make believe. And if you choose to take the role of a child, children get the benefit of taking on adult roles, of being in control and sharing their perceptions of their world, from daily irritations to profound struggles.

When four-year-old Sarah wanted to play "You're the child and I'm the grown-up," her mom—taking on the role of daughter—started begging to watch TV, a request that was sometimes an issue between them. She was surprised when her daughter said "No!" rather forcefully. Her mom increased her begging. "Please, just for one minute. Please!" she entreated. Her daughter remained firm. "No. It's not healthy for you. I like you to do healthy things." We often hear our own voices emerging from our children as they play at grown-up roles. When I was teaching preschool, I watched children play house in what we called the "dress-up corner," which consisted of a wooden stove, sink, table, various kitchen utensils, and a lot of discarded finery. I heard one of them say cheerily to the other, "Hello, dear. Would you like a gin and tonic?" It's astonishing how much of what children observe and internalize emerges during play.

Later, Sarah's mom sent me the following e-mail:

> Sarah's been interested in death lately. Recently she said, "I hope you and Daddy don't both die while we're still little girls

because then we'd have to get used to someone else." So I said, "Well, it would be Aunt Katie; that's who would take care of you if we both died." Sarah said, "Who would take care of us while Aunt Katie's on the airplane coming to get us???" I listed all the friends who live nearby who might take care of them while Katie was on her way. Anyway, since that time, her favorite game is, "Let's pretend I lost my mommy and daddy and you're my new mommy and you're telling me all about my new house and my new toys and my new little sister."

Even after all my years of playing with children, I still find it amazing and wonderful that, given a chance, children will turn instinctively to make believe as a rich and satisfying means of working on whatever challenges they may be facing.

Previous generations could take it for granted that children used their leisure time for play. We can't do that anymore. Like puffins, giant pandas, and the whooping crane, play is an endangered species. It's easy to shake our heads about the state of childhood today and wax nostalgic about yesteryear, longing for the good old days when we played outside for hours after school, when the microchip was just a twinkle in Jack Kilby's eye and Nickelodeon was what our parents and grandparents called some early version of the jukebox. We can't move backward, but for our children's sake we can't accept the status quo. Instead, we have to move forward and make a conscious, concerted effort to save make believe for future generations. The consequence of millions of children growing up deprived of play is a society bereft of joy, creativity, critical thinking, individuality, and meaning—so much of what makes it worthwhile to be human. Let's let children play. In saving make believe, we are saving ourselves.

Resources

Alliance for Childhood
www.allianceforchildhood.net
PO Box 444
College Park, MD 20741
301-779-1033

Campaign for a Commercial-Free Childhood (CCFC)
www.commercialfreechildhood.org
Judge Baker Children's Center
53 Parker Hill Avenue
Boston, MA 02120-3225
617-278-4172

International Play Association (IPA)
www.ipaworld.org/home.html
In the United States, visit: www.ipausa.org
For further information by country visit:
http:www.ipaworld.org/memberships.html

Media Center of Judge Baker Children's Center

www.jbcc.harvard.edu
53 Parker Hill Avenue
Boston, MA 02120-3225
617-278-4106

Media Education Foundation

www.mediaed.org
60 Masonic Street
Northampton, MA 01060
800-897-0089 or 413-584-8500
Fax: 800-659-6882 or 413-586-8398

National Association for the Education of Young Children

1313 L Street NW, Suite 500
Washington, DC 20005
202-232-8777

Teachers Resisting Unhealthy Children's Entertainment (TRUCE)

www.truceteachers.org
PO Box 441261
Somerville, MA 02144

Suggested Reading

Bok, Sissela. *Mayhem: Violence as Public Entertainment*. Reading: Addison-Wesley, 1998.

Cantor, Joanne. *"Mommy I'm Scared": How TV and Movies Frighten Children and What We Can Do to Protect Them*. San Diego: Harvest, 1998.

Carlsson-Paige, Nancy, and Diane E. Levin. *Who's Calling the Shots: How to Respond Effectively to Children's Fascination with War Play and War Toys*. Philadelphia: New Society Publishers, 1990.

Cordes, Colleen, and Edward Miller. *Fool's Gold: A Critical Look at Computers in Childhood*. College Park, MD: Alliance for Childhood, 2000.

Cavoukian, Raffi, and Sharna Olfman. *Child Honoring: How to Turn This World Around*. Westport, CT: Praeger Publishers, 2006.

Elkind, David. *The Power of Play: How Spontaneous, Imaginative Activities Lead to Happier, Healthier Children*. Cambridge: De Capo Press, 2007.

Erikson, Erik. *Childhood and Society.* New York: W.W. Norton, 1950.

Freud, Anna. *The Ego and the Mechanisms of Defense.* Revised edition. New York: International Universities Press, 1966.

Götz, Maya, Dafna Lemish, Amy Aidman, and Heysung Moon. *Media and the Make-Believe Worlds of Children: When Harry Potter Meets Pokémon in Disneyland.* Mahwah, NJ: Lawrence Erlbaum Associates, 2005.

Jenkinson, Sally. *The Genius of Play: Celebrating the Spirit of Childhood.* Gloucestershire, UK: Hawthorn Press, 2001.

Kasser, Tim. *The High Price of Materialism.* Cambridge, MA: MIT, 2002.

Kasser, Tim, and Allen D. Kanner, eds. *Psychology and Consumer Culture: The Struggle for a Good Life in a Materialistic Society.* Washington, DC: APA Books, 2004.

Levin, Diane E. *Remote Control Childhood? Combating the Hazards of Media Culture.* Washington, DC: National Association for the Education of Young Children, 1998.

Linn, Susan. *Consuming Kids: The Hostile Takeover of Childhood.* New York: The New Press, 2004.

Olfman, Sharna, ed. *All Work and No Play—: How Educational Reforms Are Harming Our Preschoolers.* Westport, CT: Praeger Publishers, 2003.

———. *Childhood Lost: How American Culture Is Failing Our Kids.* Westport, CT: Praeger Publishers, 2003.

Paley, Vivian Gussin. *A Child's Work: The Importance of Fantasy Play.* Chicago: University of Chicago Press, 2004.

Piaget, Jean. *Play, Dreams and Imitation in Childhood.* New York: W.W. Norton, 1962.

Postman, Neil. *The Disappearance of Childhood.* New York: Delacorte Press, 1982.

Singer, Dorothy G., and Jerome L. Singer. *The House of Make-Believe: Play and the Developing Imagination.* Cambridge, MA: Harvard University Press, 1990.

———, eds. *The Handbook of Children and Media.* Thousand Oaks, CA: Sage, 2001.

———. *Imagination and Play in the Electronic Age.* Cambridge, MA: Harvard University Press, 2005.

Thomas, Susan Gregory. *Buy, Buy Baby: How Consumer Culture Manipulates Parents and Harms Young Minds.* Boston: Houghton Mifflin, 2007.

Winnicott, Donald W. *Playing and Reality.* New York: Basic Books, 1971.

Notes

Introduction

1. Office of the United Nations High Commissioner for Human Rights, "Convention on the Rights of the Child: General Assembly Resolution 44/25," November 20, 1989, available at www.unhchr.ch/html/menu3/b/k2crc.htm (accessed July 11, 2007).

2. Tim Kasser does an excellent job of discussing materialism and happiness in his book *The High Price of Materialism* (Cambridge, MA: MIT Press, 2002). Also see Juliet Schor, "How Consumer Culture Undermines Children's Well-Being," in *Born to Buy: The Commercialized Child and the New Consumer Culture* (New York: Scribner, 2004), 141–76.

Chapter 1: Defending Pretending

1. Throughout the book, unless otherwise noted, I have changed the names and identifying characteristics of the children whose play I am describing to protect their confidentiality.

2. See Sally Jenkinson, *The Genius of Play: Celebrating the Spirit of Childhood* (Gloucestershire, UK: Hawthorn Press, 2001); David Elkind, *The Power of Play: How Spontaneous, Imaginative Activi-*

ties Lead to Happier, Healthier Children (Cambridge: De Capo Press, 2007); and Vivian Gussin Paley, *A Child's Work: The Importance of Fantasy Play* (Chicago: University of Chicago Press, 2004).

3. My colleague Diane Levin coined the term "problem-solving deficit disorder" as a condition of a modern childhood where children don't get enough time for creative play. See Barbara Meltz, "There Are Benefits to Boredom," *Boston Globe*, January 22, 2004, H1.

4. See Lev S. Vygotsky, "Play and Its Role in the Mental Development of the Children," in Jerome S. Bruner, Alison Jolly, and Kathy Sylva, eds., *Play: Its Role in Development and Evolution* (New York: Basic Books, 1976), 536–52.

5. Kathleen Roskos and Susan B. Neuman, "Play as an Opportunity for Literacy," in Olivia N. Saracho and Bernard Spodek, eds., *Multiple Perspectives on Play in Early Childhood* (Albany, NY: SUNY Press, 1998), 100–116.

6. Personal communication from Sandra Hofferth, unpublished data from two Child Development Supplements to the Michigan Panel Study of Income Dynamics, a thirty-year longitudinal survey including information on children's time use, September 15, 2006.

Chapter 2: Sold Out

1. Claire Hemphill, "In Kindergarten Playtime, A New Meaning for 'Play,'" *New York Times*, July 26, 2006, B8.

2. Donald F. Roberts, Uhla G. Foehr, Victoria Rideout, and Molly Ann Brodoie, *Kids and Media @ the New Millennium* (Menlo Park, CA: Henry J. Kaiser Family Foundation, 1999), 61.

3. An excellent discussion of television and children's imagination can be found in Dorothy G. Singer and Jerome L. Singer, *The House of Make-Believe: Play and the Developing Imagination* (Cambridge, MA: Harvard University Press, 1990), 177–98. The Singers refer to their earlier studies of *Mister Rogers' Neighbor-*

hood, which showed that the program had a positive influence on imagination.

4. See Susan Linn, *Consuming Kids: The Hostile Takeover of Childhood* (New York: The New Press, 2004), 147; and Stephen Davis, *Say Kids! What Time Is It? Notes from the Peanut Gallery* (Boston: Little, Brown, and Company, 1987), 90–97.

5. Chris Marlowe, "Verizon Adds Nick Content to Cell Phones," *Hollywood Reporter Online*, May 6, 2005.

6. Doreen Carvajal, "A Way to Calm a Fussy Baby: 'Sesame Street' by Cellphone," *New York Times*, April 18, 2005, C10.

7. Ibid.

8. Roberts, *Kids and Media @ the New Millennium*, 78.

9. Mike Shields, "Web-based Marketing to Kids on the Rise," *Media Week*, July 25, 2005, available at http://www.commercialfree childhood.org/news/webbasedmarketingonrise.htm (accessed August 14, 2005).

10. Elizabeth S. Moore, *It's Child's Play: Advergaming and the Online Marketing of Food to Children* (Menlo Park, CA: Henry J. Kaiser Family Foundation, 2006), 4.

11. For a good review of the literature on television and make believe, see Patty Valkenberg, "TV and the Child's Developing Imagination," in Dorothy G. Singer and Jerome L. Singer, eds., *Handbook of Children and the Media* (Thousand Oaks, CA: Sage Publications, 2001), 121–34.

12. Maya Götz, Dafna Lemish, Hyesung Moon, and Amy Aidman, *Media and the Make-Believe Worlds of Children: When Harry Potter Meets Pokémon in Disneyland* (Mahwah, NJ: Lawrence Erlbaum Associates, 2005).

13. See M.M. Vibbert and L.K. Meringoff, "Children's Production and Application of Story Imagery: A Cross-Medium Investigation," *Technical Report* no. 23 (Cambridge, MA: Project Zero, Harvard University, 1981). See also Patti M. Valkenberg, "Television and the Child's Developing Imagination," in Singer and Singer, eds., *Handbook of Children and the Media*, 121–34.

14. Daniel R. Anderson, "Television Is Not an Oxymoron," *Annals of the American Academy of Political and Social Science* 557 (1998): 24–38.

15. D.C. Denison, "The Year of Playing Dangerously," *Boston Globe Magazine*, December 8, 1985, 14–16, 99–107, 110.

16. Patricia Marks Greenfield et al., "The Program-Length Commercial," in Gordon Berry and Joy Keiko Asamen, eds., *Children and Television: Images in a Changing Sociocultural World* (Newbury Park: Sage Publications, 1993), 53–72.

17. Jeanne McDowell, "Pitching to Kids: Nickelodeon Is Taking Its Brands Beyond TV—A Hotel, Cell Phones, Even Cars," *Time,* August 5, 2005, A22.

18. Victoria Rideout, Elizabeth Vandewater, and Ellen Wartella, *Electronic Media in the Lives of Infants, Toddlers and Preschoolers* (Menlo Park, CA: Henry J. Kaiser Family Foundation, 2003), 28.

19. Daniel Hade, "Storyselling: Are Publishers Changing the Way Children Read?" *Horn Book Magazine* 78 (2002): 509–17.

20. Dan Anderson quoted in Barbara F. Meltz, "Marketers See Babies Noses as Pathway to Profit," *Boston Globe*, May 19, 2005, H1.

21. For a good in-depth discussion of media, media-linked toys, and their impact on children's play, see Diane Levin's work, in particular, *Remote Control Childhood? Combating the Hazards of Media Culture* (Washington, DC: National Association for the Education of Young Children, 1998). Also, Barbara Meltz, "The Best Holiday Toys Are Open-ended Ones," *Boston Globe*, December 2, 2002, H1. Several of Meltz's columns in the *Boston Globe*, for which she interviews experts in child development, have addressed the impact of commercial culture on play. See, for example, "They Don't Need Bells & Whistles" November 30, 2000, H1, and "When You Give a Toy You Endorse Values," December 2, 2004, H3.

22. Michel Marriott, "Amanda Says 'You Don't Sound Like Mommy,'" *New York Times*, August 25, 2005, C9.

23. "Toy Industry Experiences 4% Decline in Sales for the Year," *Los Angeles Times*, February 13, 2006, C6.

24. Anne D'Innocennzio, "Toy Makers Seek to Tout High-Grade Items," Associated Press, February 8, 2007 (accessed on Factiva, July 11, 2007).

25. Marriott, "Amanda Says 'You Don't Sound Like Mommy.'"

26. Edward Miller, "Dolls That Talk Too Much," *New York Times*, August 26, 2005, Letter to the Editor, A18.

27. Joan Almon, "Educating Children for a Healthy Life" (address delivered at the Sixth Annual Childhood and Society Symposium, Point Park University, Pittsburgh, Pennsylvania, June 9–10, 2006).

Chapter 3: Baby Scam

1. All three were quoted in the Campaign for a Commercial-Free Childhood press release "Stop Branding Babies: CCFC Urges Noted Public Health Organization to Get Out of the Baby Video Business," March 2006, available at http://commercialfreechild hood.org/pressreleases/sesamebeginnings.htm (accessed June 18, 2007).

2. American Academy of Pediatrics, "News Briefs," October 3, 2005, available at http://www.aap.org/advocacy/releases/oct05studies.htm (accessed July 11, 2007).

3. Victoria Rideout, *Parents, Children, and Media: A Report from the Kaiser Family Foundation* (Menlo Park, CA: Kaiser Family Foundation, 2007), 7.

4. Victoria Rideout and Elizabeth Hamel, *The Media Family: Electronic Media in the Lives of Infants, Toddlers, Preschoolers and Their Parents* (Menlo Park, CA: Kaiser Family Foundation, 2006), 26.

5. Frederick J. Zimmerman, Dimitri A. Christakis, and Andrew N. Meltzoff, "Television and TV Viewing in Children Younger than Three Years," *Archives of Pediatric and Adolescent Medicine* 161, no. 5 (2007): 473–79.

6. Ibid.

7. Rideout and Hamel, *The Media Family.*

8. Amazon.com Web site, "Toys & Games," http://www.amazon.com/ Fisher-Price-C6324-Laugh-Learn-Learning/dp/B00022F0WE/ref= pd_bxgy_t_text_b/102-4042078-5407329 (accessed July 10, 2007).

9. Rideout and Hamel, *The Media Family*, p.15.

10. Zimmerman et al., "Television and TV Viewing in Children Younger than Three Years."

11. See Daniel R. Anderson and Tiffany A. Pempek, "Television and Very Young Children," *American Behavioral Scientist* 48, no. 5 (2005): 505–22; see also Bernard G. Grela, Marina Krcmar, and Yi-Jiun Lin, "Can Television Help Toddlers Acquire New Words?" Speechpathology.com, May 17, 2004, available at http://www .speechpathology.com/Articles/article_detail.asp?article_id=72 (accessed July 10, 2006); Patricia K. Kuhl, Feng-Ming Tsao, and Huel-Mel Liu, "Foreign-Language Experience in Infancy: Effects of Short-Term Exposure and Social Interaction," *Proceedings of the National Academy of Science* 100 (2003): 9096–101.

12. Elizabeth A. Vandewater, David S. Bickham, and June H. Lee, "Time Well Spent? Relating Television Use to Children's Free-Time Activities," *Pediatrics* 117, no. 2 (2006): 181–91.

13. The Santiago Declaration and its signatories can be found at the James S. McDonnell Foundation Web site: http://www.jsmf.org/ declaration/ (accessed June 2, 2007).

14. See Laura K. Certain and Robert S. Kahn, "Prevalence, Correlates, and Trajectory of Television Viewing Among Infants and Toddlers," *Pediatrics* 109 (2002): 634–42; Dimitri Christakis and Fred Zimmerman, "Early Television Viewing Is Associated with Protesting Turning Off the Television at Age 6," *Medscape General Medicine* 8, no. 2 (2006): 63, available at http://www.medscape .com/viewarticle/531503 (accessed June 6, 2006).

15. Bruce Horovitz, "Six Strategies Marketers Use to Make Kids Want Things Bad," *USA Today*, November 22, 2006, 1B.

16. Fred Zimmerman and Dimitri Christakis, "Children's Television Viewing and Cognitive Outcomes: A Longitudinal Analysis of National Data," *Archives of Pediatrics and Adolescent Medicine* 159, no. 7 (2005): 619–25.

17. Darcy A. Thompson and Dimitri A. Christakis, "The Association Between Television Viewing and Irregular Sleep Schedules Among Children Less Than 3 Years of Age," *Pediatrics* 116, no. 4 (2005): 851–56.

18. Dimitri Christakis et al., "Early Television Exposure and Subsequent Attentional Problems in Children," *Pediatrics* 113, no. 4 (2004): 708–13.

19. Barbara A. Dennison et al., "Television Viewing and Television in Bedroom Associated with Overweight Risk Among Low-Income Preschool Children," *Pediatrics* 109 (2002), 1028–35.

20. Zimmerman and Christakis, "Children's Television Viewing and Cognitive Outcomes"; Fred Zimmerman et al., "Early Cognitive Stimulation, Emotional Support, and Television Watching as Predictors of Subsequent Bullying Among Grade School Children," *Archives of Pediatric and Adolescent Medicine* 159, no. 4 (2005): 384–88.

21. The Write News, "Teletubbies Say 'Eh-Oh' to the Internet on Their First Official Website," April 7, 2003, available at http://www.writenews.com/1998/040798.htm (accessed July 10, 2007).

22. Tom Scotney, "Eh-Oh! How Fab Four Won Over the World," *Birmingham Post*, March 31, 2007, 3 (accessed on Lexis-Nexis on July 10, 2007).

23. According to their packages, titles such as Language Nursery, Baby Beethoven, and Baby Mozart are for children ages zero to three years.

24. Anne Becker, "Billion-Dollar Babies; Can Disney's Little Einsteins teach preschoolers, Outdo Dora—and Make Money?" *Broadcast & Cable*, February 13, 2006, available at http://www.commercialfreechildhood.org/news/billiondollarbabies.htm (ac-

cessed July 10, 2007); Don Oldenberg, "Experts Rip 'Sesame' TV Aimed at Tiniest Tots," *Washington Post*, March 21, 2006, C1.

25. The Disney Company's Baby Einstein Web site: http://disney .go.com/disneyvideos/preschool/babyeinstein/ (accessed July 15, 2007).

26. Marina Krcmar, Bernard Grela, and Kirsten Lin, "Can Toddlers Learn Vocabulary from Television? An Experimental Approach," *Media Psychology* 10 (2007): 41–63.

27. Kuhl, Tsao, and Liu, "Foreign-Language Experience in Infancy."

28. Frederick J. Zimmerman, Dimitri A. Christakis, Andrew N. Meltzoff, "Associations between Media Viewing and Language Development in Children Under Age 2 Years," *Journal of Pediatrics* 151, no. 4 (2007): 364–68.

29. Personal communication with Steveanne Auerbach, "Dr. Toy," February 22, 2007.

30. For a good discussion of the development of Leapfrog, see Susan Gregory Thomas, *Buy Buy Baby: How Consumer Culture Manipulates Parents and Harms Young Minds* (New York: Houghton Mifflin, 2007), 27.

31. Lauren Foster, "Toymakers Are Looking to Technology to Give Sales a Lift," *Financial Times*, February 11, 2006, 19 (accessed on Factiva, July 11, 2007).

32. Leapfrog products Web site: http://www.leapfrog.com/Primary/ Infant / PRD_mmlearningseat / Magic+Moments153+Learning+ Seat.jsp?bmUID=1169747436746 (accessed January 26, 2007).

33. Ibid.

34. Dimitri Christakis, interview by Alison Aubry, *All Things Considered*, National Public Radio, December 14, 2005.

35. See Grela, Krcmar, and Lin, "Can Television Help Toddlers Acquire New Words?"; see also Kuhl, Tsao, and Liu, "Foreign-Language Experience in Infancy."

36. "DVD Features," Disney Baby Einstein DVD Collection—Official Baby Einstein DVD Web site: http://disney.go.com/disneyvideos/ preschool/babyeinstein/ (accessed July 16, 2007).

37. "Thomas and Friends Brand," Thomas and Friends Web site: http://www.thomasandfriends.com/usa/online_thomas_and_friends_brand_info.htm (accessed July 7, 2007).

38. Quoted in Chris Marlow, "Verizon Adds Nick Content to Cell Phones," *Hollywood Reporter Online*, May 6, 2005 (accessed on Factiva, July 10, 2007).

39. I expand on this in *Consuming Kids*, especially in chap. 2, 31–40.

40. See Thomas, *Buy Buy Baby.*

41. "Sesame Workshop 2006 Annual Report," 17, available at http://www.sesameworkshop.org/aboutus/pdf/SesameWorkshop2006.pdf (accessed July 16, 2007); "Sesame Workshop Launches New Sesame Beginnings Products at JPMA," press release, Sesame Workshop Web site: http://www.sesameworkshop.org/aboutus/inside_press.php?contentId=14223458 (accessed July 16, 2007).

42. Susan Gregory Thomas reports 750 for sale on Amazon.com in *Buy Buy Baby*, 25.

43. Don Walker, "Goo-Goo Rah Rah: Though Firm Sees a Winner in 'Baby Badger,' Critics Throw a Flag," *Milwaukee Journal Sentinel*, August 11, 2006, available at http://www.commercialfreechildhood.org/news/googoorahrah.htm (accessed September 30, 2006).

44. Baby Pro Sports Web site: http://www.babyprosports.com/ (accessed September 30, 2006).

45. "About: Research," Baby Pro Sports Web site: http://www.babypro sports.com/ research.asp (accessed September 30, 2006).

Chapter 4: True Romance

1. According to Winnicott, parents do not have to be perfect, but only "good enough." The same can be said for environments as well. See D.W. Winnicott, *Playing and Reality* (New York: Basic Books, 1971).

2. Ibid., p. 51.

Chapter 5: Michael

1. Lynette K. Freidrich-Cofer, "Environmental Enhancement of Prosocial Television Content: Effect on Interpersonal Behavior, Imaginative Play, and Self-Regulation in a Natural Setting," *Developmental Psychology* 15 (1979): 637–46.

Chapter 7: Kara

1. D.W. Winnicott. *The Maturational Processes and the Facilitating Environment* (New York: International Universities Press, 1965), 140–56.

Chapter 8: Angelo

1. See Bruno Bettelheim, *The Uses of Enchantment: The Meaning and Importance of Fairy Tales* (New York: Knopf, 1976).

Chapter 9: Wham! Pow! Oof!

1. "Transformer's Marketing More than Meets the Eye," Campaign for a Commercial-Free Childhood Web site: http://commercialfree childhood.org/transformers.htm (accessed July 8, 2007).
2. Althea Huston-Stein, Sandra Fox, Douglas Greer, Bruce A. Watkins, and Jane Whitaker, "The Effects of Action and Violence on Children's Social Behavior," *Journal of Genetic Psychology* 138 (1981): 183–91.
3. American Academy of Pediatrics, "Joint Statement on the Impact of Entertainment Violence on Children," July 26, 2000, available at www.aap.org/advocacy/releases/jstmtevc.htm (accessed July 8, 2007).
4. Center for Communication and Social Policy, *National Television Violence Study Year Three* (Thousand Oaks, CA: Sage Publications, 1998).

5. Aletha C. Huston, Edward Donnerstein, Halford Fairchild, Norma D. Feshbach, Phyllia A. Katz, John P. Murray, Eli A. Rubinstein, Brian L. Wilcox, and Diana Zuckerman, *Big World, Small Screen: The Role of Television in American Society* (Lincoln, NE: University of Nebraska Press, 1992).

6. Douglas A. Gentile and Craig A. Anderson, "Violent Video Games: The Newest Media Violence Hazard," in Douglas A. Gentile, ed. *Media Violence and Children* (Westport, CT: Praeger Publishing, 2003), 131–52.

7. NDP Group, "Report from the NPD Group Shows 45 Percent of Heavy Video Gamers Are in the Six- to 17-Year-Old Age Group," press release, September 19, 2006, available at: http://www.npd .com/press/releases/press_ 060919a.html (accessed July 11, 2007).

8. Mike Snider, "Video Games: Grand Theft Auto: Vice City," *USA Today,* December 27, 2002, D8.

9. Entertainment Software Ratings Board Web site: http://www.esrb .org/ratings/ratings_guide.jsp (accessed July 9, 2007).

10. Douglas A. Gentile and Ronald Gentile, "Violent Video Games as Exemplary Teachers," paper given at the biennial meeting of the Society for Research in Child Development, April 2005.

11 National Institute on Media and the Family, "First-Ever Summit on Video Games and Youth a Success: Medical and Health Experts Agree Video Game Violence Contributes to Aggressive Behavior in Youth," press release, November 6, 2006, available at: http://www.mediafamily.org/press/20061031.shtml (accessed July 11, 2007).

12. Federal Trade Commission Report, "Marketing Violent Entertainment to Children," April 7, 2007, available at http://www.ftc.gov/ reports/violence/070412MarketingViolentEChildren.pdf (accessed July 16, 2007).

13. John P. Murray, Mario Liotti, and Paul T. Ingmundson, "Children's Brain Activations While Viewing Televised Violence Revealed by MRI," *Media Psychology* 8 (2006): 25–37.

14. See Gerard Jones, *Killing Monsters: Why Children Need Fantasy, Super Heroes and Make-Believe Violence* (New York: Basic Books, 2003).

15. Seymour Feshbach and Robert D. Singer. *Television and Aggression: An Experimental Field Study* (San Francisco: Jossey-Bass, 1971).

16. See Diane E. Levin, *Teaching Young Children in Violent Times: Building a Peaceable Classroom* (Cambridge: New Society Publishers, 1996).

17. See the work of Diane Levin and Nancy Carlsson-Paige, *The War Play Dilemma*, 2nd ed. (New York: Teachers College Press, 2006), and *Who's Calling the Shots* (St. Paul, MN: New Society Publishers, 1987).

18. Personal communication with Marissa Clark, January 18, 2007.

19. Dafna Lemish, "The School as a Wrestling Arena: The Modeling of a Television Series," *Communication* 22, no. 4 (1997): 395–418.

20. In a letter to the Federal Trade Commission, the Campaign for a Commercial-Free Childhood reported that ads for Transformers appeared on Nickelodeon on June 25, 2007, during *Jimmy Neutron* and *Fairly Odd Parents*, both rated TVY, which means that they are suitable for children as young as two, available at http://www.commercialfreechildhood.org/pressreleases/transfor mersftcletter.pdf/08/07 (accessed July 9, 2007).

21. Personal communication with Diane Levin, November 18, 2006.

22. Ibid.

23. Albert Bandura, "Influence of Models' Reinforcement Contingencies on the Acquisition of Imitative Responses," Journal of Personality and Social Psychology 1 (1965): 589–95.

Chapter 10: The Princess Trap

1. I've always liked Bruno Bettelheim's *The Uses of Enchantment*, which takes a psychodynamic look at what fairy tales might mean

to children and how they help children grapple with developmental challenges.

2. See Joseph Campbell's commentary on the history of fairy tales in Jacob and Wilhelm Grimm, *The Complete Grimm's Fairy Tales* (New York: Pantheon, 1972), 833–64.

3. Bettelheim, *The Uses of Enchantment*, 251.

4. *The Complete Grimm's Fairy Tales*, 128.

5. Ibid., 258.

6 For an interesting discussion of the differences see Bettelheim, *The Uses of Enchantment*, 250–67.

7. Personal communication with Clint Hayashi, manager of corporate communications, Disney Consumer Products, Disney, Inc., March 9, 2007; Wendy Donahue, "Princesses Reign Supreme," *Buffalo News*, March 4, 2007, G13.

8. The film *Mickey Mouse Monopoly: Disney, Childhood and Corporate Power* (Media Education Foundation, 2001) does a really good job of discussing racism and sexism in Disney films.

9. The others are Viacom, which owns Nickelodeon, and Time Warner, which owns the Cartoon Network.

10. "Kristie Kelly for Disney Fairytale Weddings," YouTube Web site: http://www.youtube.com/watch?v=2M5WlQJCbyw (accessed July 10, 2007).

11. "Disney—Princess (2003)," Adland Web site: http://commercial-rchive.com/108397.php (accessed July 17, 2007).

12. "MGA Entertainment Introduces the Girls with a Passion for Fashion, Bratz!" *Business Wire*, June 11, 2001 (accessed on Factiva, July 11, 2007); Brent Felgner, "Bringing up Bratz; MGA Entertainment's Isaac Larian Won't Settle for Second Best," *Playthings* 104 no. 6 (June 2006) (accessed on Factiva, July 11, 2007.

13. For an interesting discussion, see Ariel Levy's *Female Chauvinist Pigs: Women and the Rise of Raunch Culture* (New York: Free Press, 2005), 9.

14. Despite product descriptions on the MGA site describing it as a "smoothie bar" (see "Bratz Formal Funk F.M. Limo," MGA Enter-

tainment Web site: http://www.mgae.com/products/new_fall_products_2003/_bratz/fmCruiserLimoBike.asp [accessed July 11, 2007]), Peter DeBenedittis points out that the glasses included distinctly resemble champagne flutes (see "Research: Alcohol Toys: Examples," Peter DeBenedittis, Media Literacy Web site: http://medialiteracy.net/purchase/ toys2.shtml [accessed July 11, 2007]).

15. Woolworth's Web site: http://www.woolworths.co.uk/ww_p2/product/index.jhtml?pid=50717538.

16. Michael Precker, "Animated Debate for Many Arab-Americans," *Dallas Morning News*, July 12, 1993, C1 (accessed on Factiva, July 11, 2007.

17. See Heather May, "Study Finds Even Toddlers Know Gender Expectations," *Salt Lake Tribune*, June 14, 2007 (accessed on Factiva, July 11, 2007; see also Kurt Kowalski, "The Emergence of Ethnic and Racial Attitudes in Preschool-Aged Children," *Journal of Social Psychology* 143, no. 6 (2003): 677–90.

18. "Disney First: Black Princess in Animated Film," MSNBC Web site: http://www.msnbc.msn.com/id/17524865/ (accessed on July 10, 2007).

19. Jayne O'Donnell, "Marketers Keep Pace with 'Tweens': Fashion-Minded Girls Prove Rich, but Fast-Moving Target," *USA Today,* April 11, 2007, B1.

20. Sharon Kennedy Wynne, "Site-Seeing with the Kids," *St. Petersburg Times*, June 29, 2007, E1; Katherine Snow Smith, "All Dolled Up," *St. Petersburg Times*, July 9, 2007, E3.

21. Rheyne Rice quoted in Reuters, "Mattel Unveils Online Barbie Community," *Los Angeles Times*, April 19, 2007, C3.

22. American Psychological Association, Task Force on the Sexualization of Girls, *Report of the APA Task Force on the Sexualization of Girls* (Washington, DC: American Psychological Association, 2007), 2, available at www.apa.org/pi/wpo/sexualization.html (accessed April 8, 2007).

23. O'Donnell, "Marketers Keep Pace with 'Tweens.'"

24. Centers for Disease Control, "Youth Risk Behavior Surveillance—

United States 2005," June 9, 2006, 78, Table 44, available at http://www.cdc.gov/mmwr/PDF/SS/SS5505.pdf (accessed on July 11, 2007).

25. See in particular David Elkind *The Hurried Child,* 3rd ed. (Reading, MA: Addison-Wesley, 2001), and *All Grown Up and No Place to Go*, 2nd ed. (Reading, MA: Addison-Wesley, 1988).

26. See Neil Postman, *The Disappearance of Childhood* (New York: Vintage, 1992).

27. Ellyn Spragins, "Out of the Classroom, Back in the House," *New York Times*, August 3, 2003, C9 (accessed on Factiva, July 12, 2007.

28. Kelli Kennedy, "College Grads Moving Back Home to Boomer Parents . . . and Staying," Associated Press, July 30, 2006 (accessed on Factiva, July 11, 2007).

29. Kid Power 2007! Web site:http://kidpowerx.com/cgibin/templates/document.html? topic=445& event=12748&document=92748# panel_can_kgoy_and_kysl_coexist (accessed July 11, 2007).

30. Personal communication with researcher Sandra Hofferth, June 2, 2005.

Chapter 11: Playing for Life

1. Walter Isaacson, *Einstein: His Life and Universe* (New York: Simon & Schuster, 2007), 13.

2. Abraham J. Heschel, *Who Is Man?* (Stanford CA: Stanford University Press, 1965), 81–93.

3. See Mihaly Csikszentmihalyi, *Flow: The Psychology of Optimal Experience* (New York: Harper Perennial, 1990).

4. Ibid., 39–40.

5. Elizabeth A. Vandewater, David S. Bickham, and June H. Lee, "Time Well Spent? Relating Television Use to Children's Free-Time Activities," *Pediatrics* 117, no. 2 (2006): 181–91.

6. Frank Rich, "Never Forget What?" *New York Times*, September 14, 2002, A15.

Chapter 12: Sasha, Your Peas Are Calling You

1. Susan Linn, "Harry, We Hardly Knew Ye (Harry Potter)," *CommonWealth*, Spring 2000, 92–94.

2. See Mary Ann Kirkby, "Nature as a Refuge in Children's Environments," *Children's Environments Quarterly* 6, no. 1 (1989): 7–12. See also Patrick Grahn, Fredrika Martensson, Bodil Lindblad, Paula Nilsson, Anna Ekman, "Ute Pa Dagis" (Outdoor Daycare), *Stad und Land* (City and Country) 145 (1997) (Hasselholm, Sweden: Norra Skane Offset).

3. Amber Mobley, "Movin' to the Music," *St. Petersburg Times*, May 17, 2007, E1.

4. See Dimitri Christakis and Fred Zimmerman, *The Elephant in the Living Room* (New York: Rodale Press, 2006).

5. I discuss this further in *Consuming Kids*, 130–31.

6. Campaign for a Commercial-Free Childhood Web site: http://www.commercialfreechildhood.org/babyvideos/ftccomplaint.htm; http://www.commercialfreechildhood.org/babyvideos/babyfirst complaint.htm (accessed July 8, 2007).

7. As this book was going to press CCFC got a letter from the FTC saying that, because Disney and Brainy Baby modified their claims and have promised not to make unsubstantiated claims about the educational benefits of their products, they saw no need to act on our complaint. The message the FTC is sending to corporations is "It's fine to deceive parents and if you're caught, promise that you won't do it again and there will be no consequences."

8. Nickelodeon's "Let's Just Play" Web site: http://www.nick.com/myworld/letsjustplay/ (accessed July 7, 2007).

9. Melanie Wakefield, Yvonne Terry-McElrath, Sherry Emery, Henry Saffer, Frank J. Chaloupka, Glen Szczypka, Brian Flay, Patrick M. O'Malley, and Lloyd D. Johnston, "Effect of Televised, Tobacco Company-Funded Smoking Prevention Advertising on Youth Smoking-Related Beliefs, Intentions, and Behavior," *American Journal of Public Health* 96, no. 12 (2006): 2154–60.

10. Frederick Zimmerman et al., "Television and DVD/Video Viewing in Children Younger than 2 years," *Archives of Pediatric and Adolescent Medicine* 161, no. 5 (2007): 473–79.

11. Allen D. Kanner and Joshua Golin, "Does Coke Money Corrupt Kids Dentistry?" *Mothering*, March/April 2005, 48.

12. See Jane Levine, Joan Dye Gussow, Diane Hastings, and Amy Eccher, "Authors' Financial Relationships with the Food and Beverage Industry and Their Published Positions on the Fat Substitute Olestra," 93, no. 4 (2003): 664–69. Accessed on Ovid July 12, 2007; Mark Barnes and Patrick S. Florencio, "Financial Conflicts of Interest in Human Subjects Research: The Problem of Institutional Conflicts," *Journal of Law Medicine and Ethics* 30, no. 3 (2002): 390–402 (accessed on Factiva, July 12, 2007); Jerome P. Kassirer, "Financial Conflict of Interest: An Unresolved Ethical Frontier," *American Journal or Law and Medicine* 27, no. 2–3, (2001): 149–79 (accessed on Factiva, July 12, 2007); and "Guideline Authors Influenced by Industry Ties, Study Says," *Drug Marketing* 4, no. 6 (2002) (accessed on Factiva, July 12, 2007).

13. Don Oldenburg, "Experts Rip 'Sesame' TV Aimed at Tiniest Tots," *Washington Post,* March 21, 2006, C1.

14. "Child's Play," editorial, *New York Times*, August 20, 2007, A18.

15. Jenna Russell, "Nature Makes a Comeback: In a Techno World, Traditional Camps Flourish," *Boston Globe*, July 7, 2007, A1.

16. For an excellent discussion of the importance of connecting to nature for children's development, see Richard Louv's *Last Child in the Woods: Saving Our Children from Nature-Deficit Disorder* (Chapel Hill, NC: Algonquin of Chapel Hill, 2006).

17. Michele M. Melendez, "Calling on Kids; Cell Phone Industry Aims at Youngest Consumers," *Grand Rapids Press*, July 3, 2005, F4.

18. Ken Heyer, a market researcher from ABI Technologies, quoted in Doreen Carvajal, "A Way to Calm a Fussy Baby: 'Sesame Street' by Cellphone," *New York Times*, April 18, 2005, C10.

Index